Free-Wheeling Easy

and around

in ^ Western Pennsylvania:

Motor-Free Trails for Cyclists, Walkers, and Cross-Country Skiers

Second Edition, with August 1997 Update

Rail-trails, greenways, towpaths, and other motor-free
bicycle touring routes in western Pennsylvania and nearby areas

Mary Shaw
Roy Weil

A portion of the purchase price of this guide supports trail development

Shaw-Weil Associates

Administrative Stuff

We are pleased to provide selected highlights on the World-Wide Web. Point your web browser at URL http://www.cs.cmu.edu/~shaw/FWE.html

On Safety, Judgment, and Personal Responsibility

We compiled this guide to support both individual trail users and the development of the trail systems. We have made a serious effort to present accurate descriptions and to confirm trail status. However, we are human, trails change with time, and we occasionally receive incorrect information. Weather, wear, construction, vandalism, changes in land status, and other forces can alter conditions, erode trail surfaces, create obstacles, or even close trails. Therefore we cannot be responsible for discrepancies between these descriptions and actual trail conditions. If you do encounter any discrepancies, please let us know.

Under no circumstances do we recommend that you trespass on private land or violate any laws. Nor do we recommend that you do anything dangerous: some trail activities have intrinsic risks, for which you must assume responsibility. Additional risks are inherent in the mix of activities that take place on the trails. Everyone who sets out on a trip assumes personal responsibility, not only for his or her own safety, but also for the safety of others on the trip. Ultimately the quality of your experience depends mostly on your own common sense and good judgment.

Table of Contents

Acknowledgments

This guide would not be possible without the trails. Most of the trails described here have come to exist only because of the dedication of many volunteers. These volunteers do everything from identifying possible routes, to negotiating land acquisition, to public relations, to trail clearing, trash removal, ongoing maintenance, sign-making, and landscaping. We thank them all. Your favorite trail has something for you to do, too.

We appreciate the support we've received from trail managers and other trail developers. Many have been generous with time and information. In particular, we thank the following for discussions, explanations, advice, and comments on draft trail descriptions: Bob McKinley of the Regional Trail Council (Yough River), Dick Wilson of Rails-to-Trails, Ed Patterson of Indiana County Parks and Laurie Lafontaine of C&I Trail Council (Ghost Town), Ron Bennett of the Butler-Freeport Community Trail Council, Bob Knepshield of the Roaring Run Watershed Association and Allegheny Valley Land Trust (Armstrong), Lynn Cochran of Allegheny Valley Trails Association, Larry Ridenour of Allegheny County Planning, Hank Parke of Somerset County Rails to Trails (Allegheny Highlands), Don Berty of the Cecil Friends of the Montour Trail, Lysle Sherwin of Loyalhanna Watershed Association (PW&S), Andy Schreffler of the Roaring Run Watershed Association, John Stephen of Friends of the Riverfront (Three Rivers), Marshall Fausold and Bill Metzger of the Montour Trail Council, Rick Galef of Salt Lick Township (Indian Creek), Tom Sexton of the PA Chapter of Rails to Trails Conservancy, Brent Wood of Metroparks Serving Summit County (OH), Debbie Ayers of Cuyahoga Valley National Recreation Area, Paul Labovitz of the National Park Service Midwest Region, Carl Rubele of the MD Dept of Transportation (Allegheny Highlands), Joanne Nelson of Peters Township (Arrowhead), Marian Crossman of Harmony Trail Council, Jack Cusick of Westmoreland Yough Trail Chapter, Chris Wagner of Yough River Trail Council, Douglas Finger of Oil Creek State Park, David Howes of the Allegheny Valley Trails Association, Jeremy Mueller of Steel Heritage Trail Council, Mick Cooper of Pittsburgh Area Cycling Coalition, and staff at Moraine and Ohiopyle State Parks. Catherine Copetas give valuable advice on production and J.W. Schoyer on marketing. Jean Weil checked the text for internal consistency. Naturally, all these folks are responsible for corrections but not for any remaining misinformation.

We also appreciate new information and suggestions from other readers, including Dave Willard of Gatto's Cycles, Carl and Cindy Benson of River's Edge Campground, Tom Kahl of Outdoor Experience, Ken of Hike n' Bike, Bob Ruppel of Riversport, Deanna Sanner, and Guy Blelloch.

Collecting information for a guide isn't quite the same thing as going out for a ride. We spent extra time driving around finding access points, we chased rumors about trails that sometimes led to unexpected riding conditions, and we rode a lot of unfinished ballast and side trails looking for trail routes. Thanks to Katherine Lynch, Don Bowman, Gordon and Jan Bugby, Weimard and Virginia McQuon, Dave and Ann Marschik, Millard and Julie Underwood, Barney Collins, George Schnakenberg, Frank and Laurie Bruns, and Kathy Ezar for putting up with all this on multiple occasions.

Freewheeling Easy

If you like to bicycle but you don't like to ride in automobile traffic or on rough, steep, undeveloped trails, this guide is for you. You will find trails for short family outings and trails for multi-day touring. If you like to walk or skate on wide smooth gentle paths, or if you're looking for easy cross-country skiing, you will also find this useful. The book provides information about trails and routes that are

⇛ easy to ride or walk,
⇛ off-limits to automobile traffic
⇛ reasonably level

Depending on their history, these routes are variously called rail-trails, bike paths, greenways, towpaths, and linear parks. Some are paved, some dirt or crushed stone; a few have short excursions onto roads with very little (and very slow) traffic. All but a very few are suitable for touring bikes with medium to wide tires and for hybrid or mountain bikes. We do include a few areas that are more challenging; they will take you to more intimate places, but they require a higher level of technical bike handling skill.

When we talk to people about these trails, their most common questions are "Is there a trail near where I live?", "How do I find that trail?", "What is the trail like?", "What facilities are there?", and "Can I buy lunch/rent a bike/swim nearby?". We have emphasized this kind of information in the trail descriptions. That's what makes this guide different from others.

Within western Pennsylvania or an easy drive into nearby regions, you will find dozens of trails that are closed to motor vehicles and are graded and surfaced for easy bicycling, walking, and similar activities. Some are short, suitable for a morning, an evening, or a short day with the family. Some are longer, good for a full day's sport touring or several days of camping.

We personally rode or walked virtually all the sections of trails that we report as developed (and many that are not). We checked almost all the trails in the first edition within the four months just before publication in early 1995. In preparation for this revision, we rechecked most of the trails during 1995. Trail conditions change with time, though, so what you find may differ. On the one hand, the trail developers may have extended the trail. On the other hand, trails deteriorate over time as a result of weather and use; they need periodic maintenance; and occasionally they are closed. Trails along rivers are susceptible to flood damage. Although we also mention a number of mountain bike areas for your convenience, we have only ridden some of them.

A number of trail development organizations are very active now, but they need continuing support. When you find a trail you enjoy, consider supporting its association; they need volunteer time and materials as well as money. Information about joining these organizations is included with the trail descriptions. They have something for you to do. Give them a call.

Finding the Way

This guide covers western Pennsylvania and nearby areas. We include most of the trails longer than 2-3 miles that are west of US219 in Pennsylvania. We also include several longer trails outside that area but still within a two and a half hour drive of Pittsburgh.

We group the trails in four clusters. The first covers trails in and around Pittsburgh, the second covers trails to the south and east, primarily the Laurel Highlands, the third covers trails to the north in the upper Allegheny River valley, and the fourth includes trails to the west and northwest at the edge of Pennsylvania and in northeastern Ohio.

We have tried to write directions so that you can find the trailheads with this book plus a state highway map. We usually begin with directions to some obvious location in the vicinity, such as a major intersection, then give detailed directions from there to each trailhead. On the trails themselves, the route is usually obvious. Bicycle routes that use roads often have extensive directions or cue sheets so you don't go astray at intersections. You won't need such instructions for these trails, because the motor-free trails have few intersections or decision points.

For extending trips, exploring nearby, or finding short-cuts to trailheads, you need more detail. We like the *Pennsylvania Atlas and Gazetteer* by DeLorme Mapping Co. It covers the entire state with topographic maps at 2.4 miles to the inch, it includes most roads, and it is good about both road names and numbers. For Pittsburgh, Allegheny County, and surrounding areas, *The Complete Atlas of Southwestern Pennsylvania and Metropolitan Pittsburgh* by Marshal Penn-York is good. Either is about $15 at many bookstores. For computer users, DeLorme also produces a CD-ROM called *Street Atlas USA* for both Macintosh and Windows, about $80. With this you can print maps of selected areas at the scale of your choice, though labeling and page segmentation are awkward.

For detailed information about the terrain, get the US Geological Service topographic maps for the area of interest. The 7.5 minute series printed at a scale of 1:24,000 or about 1" to 0.4 miles. Many outfitters and sporting goods stores now stock these maps.

The Pennsylvania Chapter of the Rails-to-Trails Conservancy publishes *Pennsylvania's Great Rail-Trails*, which gives a very brief description and sketch map for each of the 60 rail-trails that are being developed in Pennsylvania. You can find it for $12.95 at many bide shops and bookstores. You can order it from Rails-to-Trails Conservancy, PA Chapter, 105 Locust St, Harrisburg PA, 17101 (add sales tax and $4.50 for shipping). The Rails-to-Trails Conservancy publishes other guides, as well.

PennDOT publishes a free road biking map that covers the whole state. They also have detailed quadrant maps for $1.25 each or $4.50 for the set of four, plus sales tax (specify northeast, southeast, northwest, or southwest quadrant). Most of the routes on these maps are through routes on highways—sometimes busy highways. We don't find these useful, but if you want them, write PennDOT Distribution Services Unit, PO Box 2028, Harrisburg PA 17105, with check or money order made out to PennDOT Sales Store.

For information on ordering copies of this guide by mail, see page 144 (last page).

Trail Rules and Etiquette

Trail rules are mostly based on common sense. They typically include points such as:

- Non-motorized uses only. Motorized wheelchairs are permitted on many trails, and snowmobiles are permitted on only a few trails.
- Keep to right, allowing room for faster people to pass. If you stop, move off the trail; don't park bikes on the trail surface.
- When there's snow on the ground, don't walk in cross-country ski tracks and don't ski where hikers have broken the trail.
- Pass on the left after giving audible signal. Bicycles yield to other users; everyone yield to horses.
- Don't litter, dump, or otherwise misuse trail land. Carry out any litter you find.
- As guests in the neighborhood, respect the rights and privacy of landowners.
- Keep pets on leash no longer than 6'. Clean up after your pet.
- Assume horses are prohibited unless explicitly allowed.
- Bicycle riders and passengers under 12 years old *must* wear helmets (PA law).
- Trails open from sunrise to sunset only; no overnight camping, open fires, or alcoholic beverages.

If rules for a trail differ significantly from these, we note the special rules.

Pennsylvania state law now requires children under the age of 12 to wear ANSI or Snell-approved helmets when operating or riding as a passenger on a bicycle, tricycle, or similar vehicle. This law applies on motor-free trails as well as roads. Helmets are a good idea for adults, too.

Many trails have rugged, remote sections. Be prepared for both mechanical and medical problems. Go with a friend. Carry tools and a first-aid kit, and know how to use them.

Horseback riding is permitted on some trails. If horseback riding is permitted, it's usually *beside* the finished surface, not *on* it. Horses are usually excluded from picnic areas and campgrounds, except those established specifically for equestrian use.

Many trails pass close to or through private land. In some cases the relations between the trail and the neighbors are delicate. Respect the privacy and property of all nearby landowners and residents.

Multi-Use Trails

We usually bicycle these trails, so this guide is written through cyclists' eyes. The trails, however, are designed for multiple uses. Because of the very different speeds of the trail users, all must be aware of other users and provide space for them.

The trail surfaces described here range from road-quality asphalt to dirt and gravel. Some trails and some unfinished sections of trails still have the original ballast from the railroads that formerly ran there. The trail descriptions describe the predominant trail surface. Each rider must decide what range of surfaces he or she enjoys riding.

Generally speaking, if you have a racing bike with 1-inch tires, stick to the half-dozen paved trails. If you want to go far and fast, stick with ordinary roads and ride in traffic.

We swapped the tires on our old 10-speed road bikes for 1 3/8-inch touring tires with a bit more tread than the original tires. With this setup, we ride most of these trails quite happily, except for some of the "original ballast".

If you have a mountain bike or a hybrid with fat tires, you'll be able to enjoy all these trails. In some cases we mention nearby mountain biking areas for your convenience.

All of these trails are suitable for walking, hiking, and jogging as well as cycling. They provide river access for fisherfolk, and many offer excellent opportunities for birdwatching and wildlife viewing. Indeed, many copies of our first edition serve walkers.

Most of the paved trails are suitable for in-line skaters. These include Arrowhead, Oil Creek, Samuel Justus, Allegheny River, Stavich, Presque Isle, and the Emerald Necklace.

Horses are permitted on some trails. Sometimes they require special permits. These include portions of Montour, northern section of Yough River, part of C&O Canal, Ghost Town, Lower, Samuel Justus, Allegheny River, Great Shamokin Path, Butler-Freeport, and Ohio & Erie Canal. Usually they are not permitted on paved surfaces or fine packed crushed stone.

All the trails are suitable for cross-country skiers when there's enough snow. Many trail managers ask skiers and walkers to use different sides of the trail. It takes several skiers to "set" a good ski track; footprints in these tracks make skiing much harder. Parts of some trails are open to snowmobiles. Cross-country skiers should decide for themselves whether they like to ski in snowmobile tracks.

When it's possible to swim near the trail, we provide that information, as simply getting wet can make a big difference on a summer afternoon. Most of the swimming areas are unsupervised locations in rivers. They do not have lifeguards, and you use them at your own risk; we are not making a recommendation that you swim there.

How to Use this Guide

We have tried to make the descriptions easy to use. By reader request, we've kept the print size big enough for mature eyes. The typical format for descriptions includes:

- **Location map**: Approximate location of the trail on a miniature state map. The tiny bicycle shows approximately where the trail is located.
- **Description**: Narrative about the scenery and the character of the trail. Describes points of particular interest. Most of the trails are easy to follow, so you don't need detailed cue sheets.
- **Summary**: Basic information about trail, set off for reference in a special box. More details are in the text, especially about the amenities. Where we know the status of horses and snowmobiles we say what it is; if we don't have information, assume they're not permitted.
- **Detailed map**: Trail route and trailheads (access points) on a map that shows significant roads, towns, and rivers. All the maps in the book use the same scale, shown on the key below and on each map.
- **Trailheads**: First, a starting point in the *vicinity*, usually a major intersection. Then *detailed directions* to each trailhead from the starting point.
- **Amenities**: Brief information on services nearby, including rest rooms, water, bike shops, food, camping or other lodging, swimming, fishing, and winter sports.
- **Trail organization:** Trail development organization or manager.
- **Maps and guides** that tell you more about the trail or the area.

For some trails, we also describe **local history**, **attractions**, **extensions** of the route (often on roads), or **development** plans. For the major trails, the overall information appears at the beginning and separate descriptions give details about the major segments.

Map Key

━●━●━●━┥ Finished Trail(paved or unpaved)	CITY OR PLACE NAME
- - - - - - - - - - - - - Unfinished or Proposed Trail	Street Name
─────────── US or State Numbered Highway	*River or Lake Name*
─────────── Other Road	🅿 Parking area
···························· Stream	◯ State Route Number
▓▓▓▓▓▓▓▓ River or Lake	⬡ US Route Number
	⬡ Interstate Route number

Trails In and Around Pittsburgh

The Pittsburgh area will eventually be served by an outer system (Montour Trail), an inner system (Three Rivers Heritage and Steel Heritage Trails plus bikeways serving Oakland and Monroeville), and numerous individual trails connecting other parts of Allegheny County. The trail system, collectively called the Allegheny County Rail-Trails or the Greenway System, is intended to put some part of the system within walking distance of practically every county resident. In addition, plans call for connections to the major cross-country trails that will lead north and southeast from Pittsburgh.

This trail system is currently under development. Trails with completed sections include the Montour Trail, the Youghiogheny River Trail, and the Three Rivers Heritage Trail. Several more trails are in planning or engineering stages.

An engineering firm has proposed routes for the Steel Heritage Trail and the North Hills Bikeway. The Steel Heritage Trail will connect the Three Rivers Heritage Trail at Sandcastle, the Youghiogheny River Trail at McKeesport, and the Montour Trail at Clairton. It will pass through a number of landmark sites of Pittsburgh's industrial heritage. The proposed route includes 8.8 miles of separate trail, a bit less than 3 miles adjacent to roads, and a little more than 3 miles of bike lanes on roads. The North Hills Bikeway, including the Harmony Trail planned for the former interurban trolley line, will stitch together many communities of the North Hills. The proposed route for the North Hills/Harmony Trail includes 9.7 miles of separate trail, 6.3 miles adjacent to roads, and 3.9 miles of bike lanes along roads.

Trail Managers for Emerging Trails in Allegheny County

Rails to Trails and Greenways Program

Allegheny County Planning Department
441 Smithfield St
Pittsburgh PA 15222-2219
(412) 350-5960
(412) 350-5372 (fax)

Steel Heritage Trail

Jeremy Mueller
Steel Heritage Trail Council
Steel Industry Heritage Corporation
338 E 9th Av, 1st Floor
Homestead PA 15120
(412) 464-4418

Harmony/North Hills Trails

Bob Powers, Jr
Harmony Trails Council
9955 Grubbs Rd
Wexford PA 15090
Membership: $15 individual, $25 family

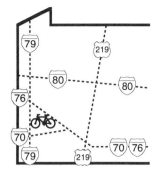

Three Rivers Heritage Trail

From Washington's Landing on Allegheny River to Sandcastle Water Park on Monongahela River via West End on Ohio River

The Three Rivers Heritage Trail will provide a close-at-hand urban outdoor experience in the form of a continuous walking path and bicycle commuting route just across the rivers from downtown Pittsburgh. Some day the trail will run 11.5 miles along the north side of the Allegheny River from Washington's Landing on the Allegheny River, through Roberto Clemente Park, past Three Rivers Stadium, across the West End Bridge, then along the south side of the Monongahela River through Station Square to Sandcastle. For now, the longest completed section runs 2.5 miles from near Washington's Landing to Carnegie Science Center. This trail, more than any other we know, breathes with the strength and vibrancy of the city. It offers vistas up and down the rivers, one of the finest views of downtown available, and close-ups of the contrast between old industry and new development on the North Side.

The northeast end of the trail is beside River Rd close to where River Rd starts up the ramp to the 30th (Washington's Landing) and 31st (Allegheny River) St Bridges. As you head toward the Point on the crushed limestone surface, for a tenth of a mile the trail is between River Rd and the river channel where rowing crews train. You can sometimes glimpse the rowers through the trees and hear the coaches calling out advice. The island ends where an unused railroad bridge crosses the road, trail and channel; note the iron ring on the downstream end of the bridge pier for tying up boats during high water. The next 0.8 mile, to the 16th St Bridge, lies between a railroad track and the Allegheny River. You'll see industrial buildings, including the Heinz plant, on the land side. Small piers, docks, and occasional benches dot the river side of the trail. Another tenth of a mile brings you to a park and overlook just upstream from Veteran's Bridge, then another tenth-mile takes you under the bridge.

Now downtown Pittsburgh towers across the river. A quarter-mile beyond Veteran's Bridge you cross the marina's launch ramp. In 0.1 mile you go under the 9th St Bridge, the first of the three identical prize-winning bridges from Downtown to the North Side. At the bridge the trail becomes paved, and the adjacent industrial area gives way to redevelopment. Soon after the 7th St Bridge, you enter the modern sculpture garden at North Shore Center. Now you join an extensive esplanade, often quite wide with seating and extensive landscaping. Pause to watch commercial traffic on the river and downtown Pittsburgh on the opposite side. Soon you cross under the 6th St Bridge to the Pittsburgh river safety building. You'll recognize it from the city seal worked out in brick on the upper facade. Here again iron rings provide anchorage in (very!) high water. This is the beginning of Roberto Clemente Park. From here it's 0.2 mile to the future Korean Veteran's Memorial and another 0.15 mile to the Vietnam Veteran's Memorial. Just before the latter, a pedestrian underpass goes to Three Rivers Stadium.

You're now across the Allegheny River from Point State Park. Here the Monongahela River joins the Allegheny to form the Ohio River. About 0.3 mile past the Three Rivers underpass, some benches allow you to enjoy the view of Point State Park and up the Monongahela River. Look the other way to watch the Duquesne Incline on the other side of the Ohio River carry passengers up and down Mt Washington. From here it's a tenth of a mile to the submarine USS Requin (that's French for "shark"), which is part of the Carnegie Science Center. The main part of the Science Center is just to your right. A final tenth of a mile brings you to the Science Center parking lot, the end of the trail for now. Eventually it will continue to the West End Bridge.

Three Rivers Heritage Trail	
Location	Along Allegheny, Ohio, Monongahela Rivers in Pittsburgh, Allegheny County
Trailheads	Washington's Landing, various points on North Side, Southside Riverfront Park
Length, Surface	Three completed sections: 1.1 mile, 2.5 mile, 0.8 mile
Character	sometimes busy, urban, sunny, mostly flat
Usage restrictions	No motorized vehicles; no snowmobiles; no horses
Amenities	Water, food, fishing
Driving time from Pittsburgh	Surrounds downtown Pittsburgh

Two other sections are open, one on Washington's Landing and one on the South Side:

A beautifully-landscaped crushed limestone trail follows the northern perimeter of Washington's Landing (formerly known as Herr's Island). This trail is only about 3' wide, so it's better suited for walking than riding. Including cross-trails, the Washington Landing trail offers 1.1 miles of pleasant strolling with views of barge traffic in the main channel and rowing in the back channel.

On the South Side, the completed asphalt trail runs 0.8 mile from 18th St to a quarter-mile upstream from the Birmingham Bridge. It is rumored that an additional 3/4 mile of heavy gravel runs from the 10th St Bridge to 18th St.

Although these completed segments don't yet provide enough trail for a full-day bike trip, they offer excellent close-to-town walking opportunities or short family excursions.

Development plans

Friends of the Riverfront maintains and improves the existing rail through monthly volunteer activities. They are working on connections to complete the trail from Washington's Landing down the Allegheny River, across the West End Bridge, and up the Monongahela River to Sandcastle. This trail provides an anchor for eventually creating a much-needed transportation link. The Steel Heritage Trail will connect the Sandcastle end of the Three Rivers Heritage Trail to the Youghiogheny River Trail at McKeesport and the Montour Trail near Clairton. A link between the West End Bridge and the Coraopolis trailhead of the Montour Trail has also been proposed The flood of Jan 1996 left mud and debris from 30th St to 9th St. This should be cleaned and repaired by summer 1996.

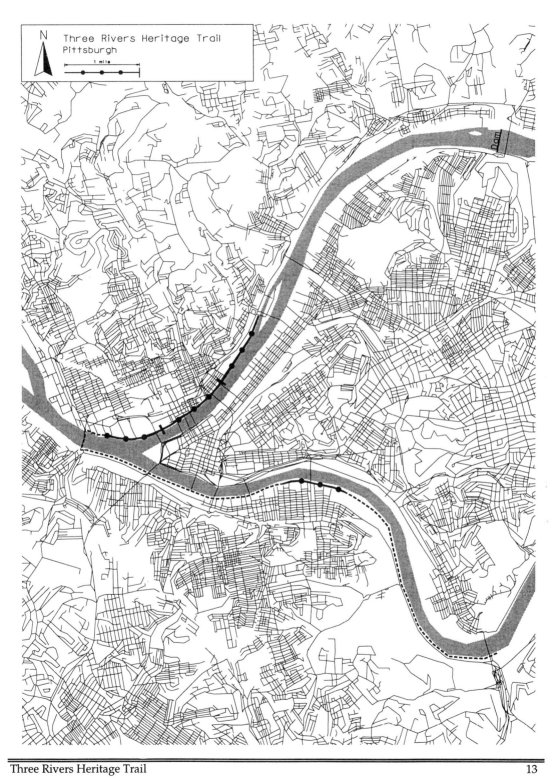

Three Rivers Heritage Trail
Pittsburgh

1 mile

Access points

Washington Landing: From PA28 (East Ohio St), turn onto the 31st St bridge, then immediately right at the traffic light onto a ramp, then immediately left at the next traffic light onto the 30th St bridge, which takes you onto Washington Landing. Turn left when the road does, and continue at least under the 31st St bridge. At this point you're inside the trail loop. Park any legal place. If you continue to the northern end of the road, watch out for the strategically hidden stop sign under the railroad bridge.

North Side: For the eastern end, use legal street parking in the neighborhood. During business hours, Washington Landing is preferred; on-street parking or Riverfront Commons is better on weekends. For the western end, use parking for Three Rivers Stadium or Carnegie Science Center.

Southside Riverfront Park: From East Carson St, turn toward the river on 18th St. Follow the road across the tracks and upstream to parking just past the boat ramp under the Birmingham Bridge. Note that they do ticket trailerless cars parked in trailer spaces.

Amenities

Rest rooms, water: Occasional water fountains. No public rest rooms.

Bike shop, rental: Many bike shops in the area, but none adjacent to the trail.

Restaurant, groceries: Off the trail on the North Side or in Pittsburgh. The Strip District, just across the 16th St bridge, is a mecca for both buying and eating food.

Camping, simple lodging: No camping. Hotels in town. The Priory B&B nearby on the North Side.

Swimming, fishing: This section of the Allegheny has a lot of power boat traffic, both commercial and recreational. The water is unappealing for swimming, and the currents can be treacherous. There are lots of fishing spots between the trail and the river.

Winter sports: There's probably too much foot traffic for XC skiing. No snowmobiles.

Trail organization

John Stephen
Friends of the Riverfront
PO Box 42434
Pittsburgh PA 15203
(412) 488-0212
Annual membership: $10 limited income, $25 individual, $40 family

Maps, guides, other references

There are many guides to the city of Pittsburgh. A good street map will help.

USGS Topographic Maps: Pittsburgh East, Pittsburgh West

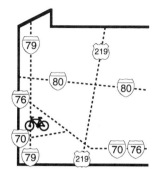

Montour Trail

Coraopolis to Clairton in Allegheny and Washington Counties

The abandoned rights-of-way of the Montour and the Peters Creek Branch railroads make a sweeping crescent around the western and southern suburbs of Pittsburgh, dipping back and forth between Allegheny and Washington Counties. The Montour Trail system follows this route and will eventually offer 54 miles of trail, amounting to 47 miles of main line and 7 miles of spurs. It runs from Coraopolis on the Ohio River to Clairton on the Monongahela River. From Coraopolis along Montour Run to Imperial the trail is primarily rural except for the area near the Parkway. From Imperial south and west, under US22 into Washington County south to McDonald then east to Cecil, it's extremely rural and agricultural, with some restored strip mines. As it enters Peters Township and approaches US19 it becomes suburban residential until it reenters Allegheny County near South Park. From South Park to Clairton it's again more rural.

Three sections are now open: Moon-Robinson-Findlay-North Fayette, Cecil, and Arrowhead (Peters Township). Together they cover 20.4 miles. Most of the trail will be crushed limestone, some parts with a parallel dirt treadway for horses. Peters Township is developing the Arrowhead Trail in asphalt. The segments of trail and their status are:

Robinson-Moon-Findlay-N Fayette	11.5 miles	finished (crushed limestone)
Robinson/Mt Pleasant	13.2 miles	development to start 1996
Westland Mine Spur	3.5 miles	unimproved
Cecil	5.7 miles	finished (crushed limestone)
Muse Spur	~2 miles	unimproved
Cecil/Arrowhead Gap	2.2 miles	unimproved
Arrowhead	3.2 miles	finished (asphalt)
Bethel Park Spur	3.0 miles	unimproved
South Park	~6 miles	development to start 1996
Jefferson	~5 miles	unimproved

In a public/private partnership, Montour Trail Council and Allegheny County will have easements or ownership of the 28 miles of trail within the county (including 10 miles yet to be acquired). The Montour Trail Council owns 21 miles within Washington County. Peters Township owns a 6-mile segment. The Montour Trail Council's goal is to open the entire trail by 1998.

Development plans

The Montour Trail Council holds regular volunteer trail development activities, both for improving the established segments and for preparing new segments for development.

Plans to extend and improve the currently-open trail segments are described with those segments. In addition, the Montour Trail Council expects to complete a 2-mile section between Stewart and Triphammer Roads near South Park in 1996. The trail council is also acquiring land and easements for other planned sections.

Maps, guides, other references

Trail Users' Guide to The Montour Trail. Trail map/brochure available at trailheads and local bike shops.

Trail organization

Montour Trail Council
PO Box 11866
Pittsburgh PA 15228-0866

(412) 257-2328 for voicemail system
(412) 831-2030 for information

Membership: $15/year individual, $25/year family

Robinson-Moon-Findlay-North Fayette Section

Along Montour Run from near Coraopolis on the Ohio River to west of Imperial in Allegheny County

The longest completed segment of the Montour Trail is the westernmost, running from mile 0 near Coraopolis to mile 11.5 west of Imperial. This segment follows Montour Run, beginning near the Ohio River, passing under the Parkway West to Imperial, then continuing west along South Fork Montour Run to a point near the intersection of US22 and PA980 at the Allegheny County line. It's finished in crushed limestone, 10 feet wide.

The trail begins near Coraopolis, at Groveton by Montour Run under the PA51 bridge. From here to Beaver Grade Rd (mile 3.2), the trail runs largely through woods alongside Montour Run, punctuated occasionally with single houses. You'll also see a few industrial sites: a superfund site (mile 0.3), Snyder's scrap metal (mile 0.6), and Moon Township Water Pollution Control Plant (mile 1.3), which smells like most sewer plants.

At mile 1.7 the trail passes through the Forest Grove Sportsman's Association. Shooting ranges occupy both sides of the trail, so exercise caution here and stay on the trail. From Beaver Grade Rd (mile 3.2) to Cliff Mine (mile 5.9), the trail is within sight (and sound) of Montour Run Rd and Cliff Mine Rd on one side, but the other is all woods. In this section the trail crosses Montour Run three times. It also crosses the roads to Robinson Town Centre and two other commercial parking lots.

Montour Trail, Moon-Robinson-Findlay-North Fayette Section	
Location	Along Montour Run in Robinson, Moon, Findlay and North Fayette Townships, Allegheny County
Trailheads	Groveton, Montour Run Exit of Parkway, Enlow, near BFI landfill
Length, Surface	11.5 miles, crushed limestone
Character	Uncrowded, rural to wooded, mixed shade and sun, flat
Usage restrictions	Horses ok on grass—stay off improved surface; no motorized vehicles; no snowmobiles
Amenities	Water, restaurant, groceries
Driving time from Pittsburgh	30 minutes west

At Cliff Mine (crossing Steubenville Pike-Enlow Rd), the trail passes behind a scrap yard and some houses then crosses Cliff Mine Rd (mile 6.2). Here the trail works away from roads into the woods, crossing Montour Run four times before entering the 558-foot Enlow Tunnel (mile 7.2-7.3). Just west of the tunnel, cattails grow in a small wetland (mile 7.5). The trail emerges at the old Enlow ballfield just before the Five Points intersection (mile 8), where it crosses Montour Run twice more. Go early on a summer morning to watch the rabbits.

After Five Points, the trail runs in a short cut full of wildflowers, then enters the outskirts of Imperial with houses on the east and a construction yard on the west. Soon it parallels the streets of Imperial. From the embankment you can look down onto the shopping district and future railroad museum along Main St or up on the other side to the houses along Station St. After crossing the trestle over US30 (mile 8.9) the trail enters a residential area, then reclaimed strip mines. A farm with fine barn provides visual relief (mile 11.1). The finished trail currently ends at mile 11.5, near the BFI Imperial landfill.

Local history, attractions

The Montour Railroad was started in 1877 to haul coal from Mifflin and Library to the Ohio River. It also hauled general goods. Bridges on this section are dated 1924. The Montour Railroad was gradually abandoned between 1962 and 1984.

The BFI Imperial Sanitary Landfill near mile 11.5 offers tours. Call (412) 695-0900.

Enlow Tunnel, mile 7.2

Extensions of the ride

There is good mountain bike riding between Montour Run Rd and Robinson Town Centre. This includes a fairly level track parallel to the trail and a considerable amount of steep technical single-track. One of the trailheads is across Montour Run Rd from Brothers Grimm Lounge (mile 3.1), near the parking lot entrance of the blue factory.

A 9-mile loop on lightly-traveled roads offers an alternative at the south end of the trail. This loop begins at trail mile 8, Five Points intersection near Enlow ballfield, and ends at trail mile 11.5, the BFI trailhead. At Five Points, take Old 978 away from the trail. This road was orphaned by airport construction and has almost no traffic. After 0.8 miles, take the left fork to stay out of the airport operations area. Two miles later, the road swings back toward the Parkway and the surface turns to gravel. At 2.9 miles from Five Points, take the right (larger) fork across a bridge. This road ends at a stop sign on SR3089 (Moon-Clinton Rd), 4.3 miles from Five Points. Turn left on SR3089 and go a block to the highway department maintenance yard on the left, just before SR3089 starts uphill. Turn left, pass the maintenance yard, and turn right on a narrow residential road. Follow this road up the hill to the intersection with US30 and SR3089 at Clinton. Mamone's restaurant has good soup; try the tomato-potato, but on Sunday don't arrive before 1:00 PM. There's also a convenience store here. Cross US30 and continue on SR3089 (now called Washington Rd). Just past the post office take the left fork down the hill to stay on SR3089 with light traffic. Follow SR3089 (1.7 miles downhill!) to a stop sign at SR3071 (Potato Garden Rd). Turn left on SR3071, follow rolling hills 2.5 miles to SR3070 (Boggs Rd) and turn left again. This intersection is not obvious—you'll cross a bridge toward the BFI Imperial Sanitary Landfill. Soon after the turn, go straight into the Montour Trail at the parking lot (mile 11.5) just as the road starts left up a small hill.

Development plans

The Montour Trail Council holds titles or easements to the right-of-way between Imperial and the Cecil segment. In early 1996, the Montour Trail Council was planning the continuation from the BFI Imperial terminus southward 6 miles to McDonald. This will leave a gap of only about 7 miles between this segment and the Cecil segment.

At the other end of the trail, there is a possibility of extending the trail from Groveton (mile 0) back to Coraopolis. This would provide access to the amenities in Coraopolis.

The Hollow Oak Land Trust is developing an extensive greenway along Montour Run. The trail will follow the spine of the greenway, which will also include some tributaries.

Access points

Vicinity: Directions begin at the interchange of I279/US22/US30 (Parkway West) with I79. To reach this point from Pittsburgh, go west on I279/US22/US30 (Parkway West).

Northeast trailhead (Groveton): At the intersection of I279/US22/US30 with I79, go north on I79 to Exit 17, PA51. Exit northbound on PA51. After less than half a mile, PA51 crosses Montour Run on a high bridge. Immediately after crossing the bridge, make an extremely sharp right onto Montour Rd. The intersection is marked with a large sign for H. Snyder Scrap and a small sign for Montour Trail. Go 0.1 mile on Montour Rd to trailhead parking under the PA51 bridge. Park well clear of the narrow road.

Parkway trailheads (Montour and Cliff Mine): At the intersection of US22/30 with I79, continue west on the Parkway for 5.8 miles (it will change number to PA60). Exit onto Montour Run Rd at Exit 2. *For Montour trailhead:* At Exit 2, follow signs for Montour Run Rd. Just after you get clear of the intersection, there is plenty of parking on the wide shoulder of Montour Run Rd within sight of the trail. You will be on the north side of the Parkway near the entrance to Wickes Furniture. *For Cliff Mine trailhead:* Follow the

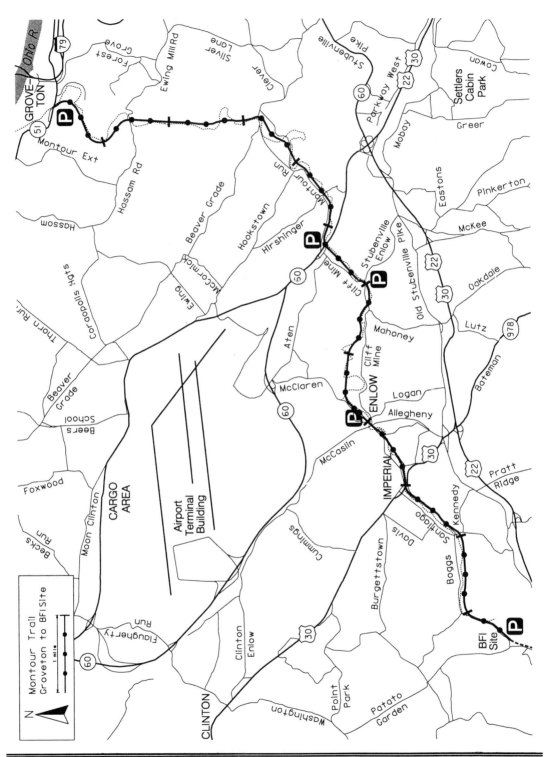

Free-Wheeling Easy in Western Pennsylvania

signs from Exit 2 to Cliff Mine Rd and follow Cliff Mine Rd about a mile to parking at the intersection with Steubenville Pike-Enlow Rd.

Enlow trailhead: At the intersection of US22/30 with I79, continue west on the Parkway for 7.9 miles (it will change number to PA60). After passing the Montour Exit, follow PA60, the Airport Expressway, rather than Business 60. Exit onto McClaren Rd at Exit 4, following signs for Imperial. Go 1.5 miles to parking at Enlow ballfield, just before Five Points (the first major intersection).

Boggs Road (BFI) trailhead: At the intersection of US22/30 with I79, continue west on the Parkway for about 3.8 miles. At the interchange with PA60, exit westbound on US22/30. Continue westbound on US22 for about 6.8 miles, staying on US22 where US30 splits off. Take the PA980 exit and go north on SR3071 for about half a mile. Turn right across a bridge on SR3070 (Boggs Rd) toward the BFI landfill. Shortly after the turn, go straight into trailhead parking instead of following the road slightly left up the hill.

Amenities

Rest rooms, water: Seasonal portable toilets at most trailheads. The Sportsman's Club at mile 1.7 offers the courtesy of their rest rooms. Seasonal water fountain below Robinson Town Centre, at the trail crossing near the intersection of Park Manor Blvd and Montour Run Rd.

Bike shop, rentals: None yet. Some basic bike parts at K-Mart (uphill west from Montour Run Rd) and in Robinson Towne Centre (uphill east from Montour Run Rd).

Restaurant, groceries: In Coraopolis, but it's a mile or so on a busy road with poor shoulders. Brothers Grimm Lounge near mile 3.1. In Robinson Town Centre on top of the hill near the Parkway, accessible from mile 4.2 on a narrow, busy road. Schmidt's Restaurant near mile 5.8 may or may not be open (let us know). Two bars (both closed on Sunday), a pizza carryout, and a grocery store at mile 8.9 near the trestle in Imperial; a pedestrian tunnel under the trail at mile 8.6 (there's a sign for this side trail) may help you get there.

Camping, simple lodging: None

Swimming, fishing: Swimming depends on whether you're willing to swim in Montour Run. There are a few spots that may be deep enough, but the water quality may discourage you. Lower Montour Run is stocked with trout by the Sportsman's Club.

Winter sports: Cross-country skiing is encouraged. Snowmobiles are prohibited.

Maps, guides, other references

Trail Users' Guide to The Montour Trail. Trail map/brochure available at trailheads and local bike shops.

USGS Topographic Maps: Oakdale, Ambridge, Clinton. Midway and Canonsburg required for undeveloped section to Cecil.

Cecil Township Section

Cecil Township Park to Hendersonville in Washington County

After a 13.2-mile gap from Imperial, the Montour Trail resumes behind Cecil Township Park. To reach the trail there, start from Cecil Park on the south side of PA50. This is actually in Venice. From here it runs 4.3 miles to Hendersonville and an additional 1.4 miles to Chartiers Creek. The trail itself is crushed limestone 10 feet wide, except in the tunnel. It is complemented by extensive signage and landscaping.

Behind the tennis courts in Cecil Park a footbridge crosses the creek into a small glade. At the opposite end of this glade a path rises from left to right to meet the rail-trail at grade level at mile 24.7. From here the trail passes eastward through the domestic suburbs of Cowden (mile 25.4) and Bishop (mile 26.1). Swinging away from residential development, you enter the cut that leads to the curved National Tunnel (mile 27 to 27.1). This major feature of the trail is 633 feet long, at an elevation of 1138'. The trail in the tunnel is loose ballast to improve drainage, so cyclists should be prepared to dismount and walk. Past the tunnel the cut opens up and the trail runs through open farms and woods. Four and a half miles east of Cecil Park the trail is interrupted at Hendersonville (mile 29.1), where the bridge over SR1009 (Washington Pike on maps, Morganza Rd on the ground) is missing. To continue, descend to road level and cross carefully. You used to be able to get ice cream at The Hendersonville Shops, also called "the company store", just across the intersection. This property was sold in 1995, and the new owner is trying to re-open the store.

Picking up again behind The Hendersonville Shops (use the driveway on the far side of the building), the trail continues east for another 1.4 miles to the trestle over Chartiers Ck. The trestle is undecked, fenced off, and closed. The section of the trail from Hendersonville to the trestle was opened in fall 1995. At that time the surface was still rough; the trail council expects to install a crushed limestone surface in spring 1996. Eventually the trail will continue from here to Arrowhead Trail in Peters Township.

Montour Trail, Cecil Township Section	
Location	Cecil Township, Washington County
Trailheads	Cecil Township Park, Dacor Dr, McConnell Rd, Hendersonville
Length, Surface	5.7 miles; 4.3 in crushed limestone, additional 1.4 miles to be surfaced spring 1996
Character	Busy, suburban to wooded, sunny, flat
Usage restrictions	Horses ok on grass—stay off improved surface; no motorized vehicles; no snowmobiles
Amenities	Rest rooms, water
Driving time from Pittsburgh	35 minutes south-southwest

Extensions of the ride

From the eastern end of the trail 1.4 miles past Hendersonville, the trail will eventually continue 2 miles to the western end of the Arrowhead trail. However, another tunnel, two closed and fenced high trestles, two more missing bridges, and a poor crossing for US19 (all in the space of 2 miles) currently prevent a direct trail link. Instead, you can connect from Hendersonville to Arrowhead Trail on roads, but you'll have to deal with hills and traffic. Here's how: From Hendersonville, follow the road parallel to the trail (it's Hahn on maps, Georgetown on the signs) for 0.3 miles east; turn left to pass under the trail, go 0.8 miles, then turn right at the T intersection (Baker Rd). Follow this road for about 3 miles past the Greenmoor Riding School, down the hill through Lawrence (also called Hill Station), under US19, to Pelipetz Rd. The road becomes Valley Brook Rd as you cross Chartiers Creek between Lawrence and US19. At Pelipetz Rd, 0.5 mile after you cross under US19, turn right to the Arrowhead trailhead. Be careful in traffic on Valley Brook Road, especially near US19.

National Tunnel, mile 27

Development plans

The missing bridge at Hendersonville will be replaced soon, and the trail east of Hendersonville will get its trail surface and fencing early in 1996. Peters Township plans to complete the connection between this section and the Arrowhead trail eventually.

At the other end of the trail, westbound from Cecil Park, two bridges need extensive work before the trail can be extended the half-mile to the intersection of PA980 with PA50 in Venice.

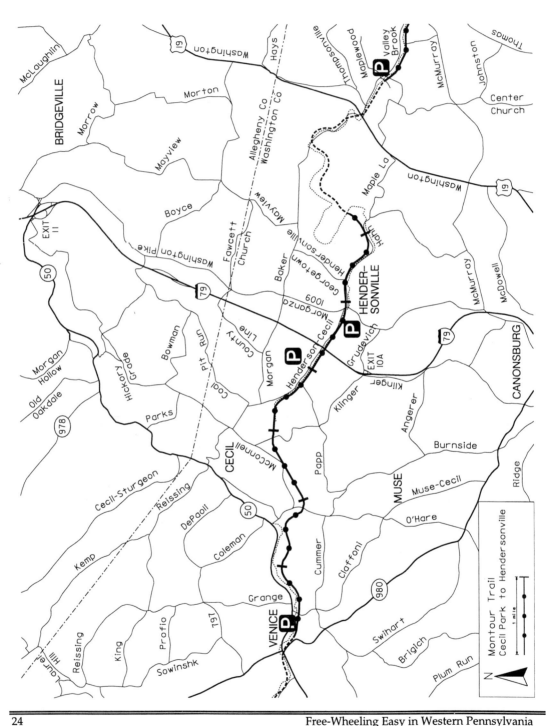

Montour Trail
Cecil Park to Hendersonville

1 mile

N

Access points

Vicinity: Directions begin headed south from I279/US22/US30 (Parkway West) on I79 toward the Bridgeville Exit (Exit 11, PA50). To reach this point from Pittsburgh, go west on I279 and turn south on I79.

West trailhead (Cecil Park): From I79, take the Bridgeville Exit (Exit 11, PA50) and go west on PA50 6.7 miles to the Cecil Township park. The park is actually in Venice, 2.7 miles west of Cecil, on the south side of the road. On weekends, please park in the township building parking lot, leaving park parking for park users.

Dacor Drive trailhead: From I79, take the Bridgeville Exit (Exit 11, PA50) and go west on PA50 5.5 miles, past Bishop. Turn south on Dacor Drive and go 0.25 mile to the parking area.

McConnell Rd trailhead: From I79, take the Bridgeville Exit (Exit 11, PA50) and go west on PA50 4.9 miles to Bishop. Turn south on Muse-Bishop Rd, then left (east) on McConnell Rd. The parking area is just over half a mile east of this intersection.

East trailheads (Kurnick and Hendersonville): From I79, take the Southpointe-Hendersonville exit (Exit 10A). At the bottom of the ramp, turn left (east) and follow signs to Hendersonville. The signs will lead you east for 0.5 mile to SR1009 (Morganza Rd), then left (north) on Morganza Rd for 0.5 mile to the Hendersonville trailhead. For this trailhead, turn left at the Hendersonville Shops, just *before* the road goes through the cut where a bridge once carried the railroad and a new bridge will eventually carry the trail. For additional parking at the Kurnick lot, turn left on SR1010 (Hendersonville-Cecil Rd) just *after* the road goes through the cut where a bridge once carried the railroad. Follow Hendersonville-Cecil Rd 0.8 mile to the Kurnick parking area on the left.

Amenities

Rest rooms, water: Rest rooms and water at Cecil Park in season. Portable toilets all year at Cecil Park and seasonally at the Kurnick parking lot and the ball field near Hendersonville.

Bike shop, rentals: None

Restaurant, groceries: Convenience stores along PA50 in Cecil (traffic, alas). Hope that the Hendersonville Shops reopen some day.

Camping, simple lodging: None

Swimming, fishing: None

Winter sports: Cross-country skiing is encouraged. Snowmobiles are prohibited.

Maps, guides, other references

Trail Users' Guide to The Montour Trail. Trail map/brochure available at trailheads and local bike shops.

USGS Topographic Maps: Canonsburg.

Arrowhead Trail

Town of McMurray in Washington County

This popular trail runs through residential areas of Peters Township. Frequent informal side routes provide access to local communities. Expect lots of company on the trail, including pedestrians, dog-walkers, and roller-bladers. It's well laid out, with a good asphalt surface and extensive landscaping. The northern portion is 11' wide; the southern end 8'. There is so much traffic that a striped center line has been added to remind people to stay right. Although essentially flat, the trail has enough curves and alternations between residential and wooded areas to remain interesting. Trees keep it reasonably well shaded. Considering the amount of development nearby, the trail feels very rural.

The only section of the Montour trail under separate management and the first to open, the Arrowhead Trail is being developed and managed by Peters Township. It currently includes approximately miles 33 to 36 and will be extended at both ends.

From the western parking lot at Pelipetz Rd, an access ramp goes under the trail and curls up to meet the trail at the end of the pavement. You begin in woods, separated from Valley Brook Rd by Brush Run, and climb gradually to McMurray, picking up residential development along the way. By the time you reach McMurray you'll know you're in the suburbs. Just after crossing over McMurray Rd you pass the trailside Hike n' Bike shop. You remain in the suburbs until Bebout Rd, where the right side of the trail gives way to Peterswood Park. You'll pass a spur trail that climbs up to the Peterswood playing fields. After crossing Sugar Camp Rd, you reach Library Jct, where an unpaved spur branches right (east) and the paved trail climbs briskly to the parking lot on Brush Run Rd.

Arrowhead Trail	
Location	Peters Township, Washington County
Trailheads	Pelipetz Rd, Brush Run Rd
Length, Surface	3.2 miles developed, 6 miles planned; asphalt 8-11 feet wide
Character	Busy, urban, shady, flat
Usage restrictions	No motorized vehicles; no snowmobiles; no horses; 20 mph limit for bicycles
Amenities	Rest rooms, water, bike rental, food
Driving time from Pittsburgh	45 minutes south-southwest

Local history, attractions

The Montour Railroad was organized in 1877 to haul coal from Mifflin and Library to the Ohio River. It also hauled general goods on the route. This section was built in 1912-1914. It was transferred to the P&LE in 1975, abandoned in 1977, and acquired by Peters Township in 1985 for development as a multi-use recreational trail

Extensions of the ride

A paved spur trail starts across the trail from the handicapped parking lot. It takes you up the hill into Peterswood Park. In the park it makes 1.2-mile loop past the soccer fields, playground, and baseball field.

The future continuation of the Montour Trail will leave the paved trail at Library Jct on the route now marked as "Walking Trail". It currently extends 1.7 miles before ending at the fenced-off trestle over Library Rd, which now has neither deck nor railing.

The trail is near Pittsburgh, so all the nearby roads are likely to carry traffic.

Development plans

Planned widening and construction of the Valley Brook-McMurray intersection will require replacement of the trail bridge; the trail may be interrupted here for a few weeks.

The trail will continue west from Pelipetz Rd to near US19 (soon) to connect with the Cecil section at Hendersonville (eventually). Extension past US19 will require extensive construction: three bridges over Brush Run, a good crossing for US19, two high trestles (now fenced off), and a tunnel.

From Library Jct the trail will extend east to meet the rest of the Montour Trail as it re-enters Allegheny County west of South Park. The future Bethel Park spur will go 3.0 miles from the Brush Run Rd parking lot to the corner of Logan and Irishtown Rds.

Access points

Vicinity: Directions begin headed east on Valley Brook Rd (SR1010) from its intersection with US19. To reach this point from Pittsburgh, go south on US19. About 1.8 miles past Boyce Rd, or 1 mile past the Allegheny/Washington County line, or the third traffic light past the county line turn left on the ramp, then left at stop sign on Valley Brook Rd (SR1010) toward McMurray.

West trailhead (Pelipetz): After turning from US19 on Valley Brook Rd (SR1010), continue 0.5 mile and turn right on Pelipetz at the intersection of Valley Brook Rd with Pelipetz Rd and Maplewood Dr. The parking area appears almost immediately on the left.

East trailhead (Brush Run): After turning from US19 on Valley Brook Rd (SR1010), continue about 1.5 miles to SR1002 (McMurray Rd) and turn left. Go about 1.4 miles and turn right on SR1004 (Brookwood Rd). Go about 0.9 miles and turn left on Brush Run Rd (T757). The trailhead parking lot is on the right, just past Scott Rd.

Other access: Along Valley Brook Rd (SR1010), there is pedestrian access at McMurray Rd (SR1002), bike access at the bike shop just east of McMurray, and pedestrian access at Bebout Rd. There is bicycle and pedestrian access via the spur trail in Peterswood Park.

Amenities

Rest rooms, water: Rest rooms at the playground in Peterswood Park. The Hike n' Bike shop offers use of their rest room to trail users.

Bike shop, rentals: Hike n' Bike, along trail just east of E McMurray Rd.

Restaurant, groceries: Deli/grocery a block from the trail at McMurray Rd near the intersection with Valley Brook Rd. Be careful at this busy intersection.

Camping, simple lodging: Motels along US19 or at exits of nearby I79.

Swimming, fishing: None

Winter sports: No snowmobiles. Cross-country skiing only when snowfall is 4" or more.

Trail organization

Peters Township owns and independently operates this part of the Montour Trail.

    Joanne F. Nelson, Director
    Peters Township Department of Parks and Recreation
    610 East McMurray Rd
    McMurray PA 15317
    (412) 942-5000

Maps, guides, other references

Arrowhead Trail. Trail map/brochure from Peters Township

Trail Users' Guide to The Montour Trail. Trail map/brochure available at local bike shops.

USGS Topographic Maps: Bridgeville. Glassport for undeveloped section to Clairton.

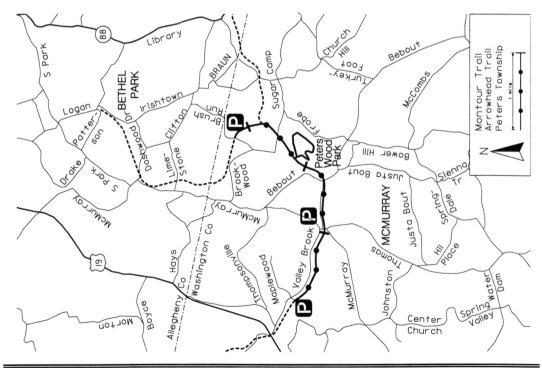

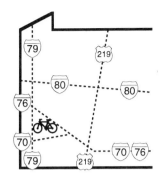

Shorter Trails and Bike Lanes

In addition to the trails that get you away from roads, several areas of Pittsburgh offer bike lanes that provide some separation from traffic. Bike lanes are established along Beechwood Blvd in Point Breeze and Squirrel Hill, and also in Riverview, North, and South Parks. A short trail in Schenley Park has been developed on the former bridle trails; this one is separated from motor vehicle traffic (except for the Humvee that passed us while we were cross-country skiing one winter).

Most of these trails are in parks run by Allegheny County and the City of Pittsburgh.

Schenley Park Trails

Park Loop on Former Bridle Trails, Schenley Park

Nearly two miles of the Schenley park trail system have been finished in packed crushed limestone. This makes a good surface for most bicycles. The trail forms a loop that begins and ends near the only traffic light in Schenley Park. Begin just south of the intersection where Overlook Dr ends on Greenfield Rd. Drop gently down the hill and bear right into the woods. You'll be on a gentle downhill that has great views to the south, overlooking the Parkway. You emerge at a 3-point trail junction near the swimming pool (fee); this is the midpoint of the trail. Right takes you to the pool; left takes you down a short slope to pass under the Blvd of the Allies bridge. Go left here. After going under the Blvd of the Allies you'll swing right, get a look down at Panther Hollow Lake, pass the entrance to a small parklet, and cross under Panther Hollow Bridge (the one with the panther statues). After 1.9 miles you'll reach another 3-point trail junction. The right branch takes you into the picnic area next to the traffic light where you started.

Other, rougher, trails are also available. For example, at the 3-point trail junction at the end of this ride, you can continue another mile in the park to Panther Hollow Lake instead of returning to the traffic light. This trail, however, is dirt and sometimes rutted.

Access points

There is only one traffic light in Schenley Park. It's at the intersection of Greenfield Rd, Hobart St, Bartlett St, and Panther Hollow Rd (which you probably think is the extension of Boulevard of the Allies into the park). It's actually a simple intersection, but everything changes names here. This is the best access point for the trail, as there is no other road crossing. Overlook Drive runs into Greenfield Rd just south of this intersection. You can park on Overlook Drive or Bartlett St.

There is also some parking and trail access at the playground at the midpoint of the trail. This is near the intersection of Panther Hollow Rd and Blvd of the Allies

Beechwood Blvd Bike Lanes

Along Beechwood Blvd from Fifth Av to Browns Hill Rd

Signs and white lines along Beechwood Blvd set off the both sides of the road as bicycle lanes. Beechwood Blvd takes you through several traditional Pittsburgh neighborhoods, including some quite fine homes. For the most part it is wide enough for cars and bikes to co-exist. It runs almost entirely in residential areas.

The bike lanes start at 5th Av at the tennis-court entrance to Mellon Park. They wind along Beechwood Blvd for 4.0 miles up and down hill across Forbes, along the edge of Frick Park, over Squirrel Hill, and down to the intersection with Browns Hill Rd. Unfortunately, the bike lanes also serve for parking. Unless you're collecting driver-side car doors, this is not an advantage.

Extensions

Along Beechwood Blvd you'll pass Frick Park Parklet, with playground. You can ride into the playground along the fitness course. At the bottom of the sled riding bowl, you can enter a network of mountain biking trails. Alternatively, you can follow the paved trail in the playground to the end of the pavement and continue on a gravel trail into the "roller coaster", the most difficult single-track mountain biking trail in the park.

Access points

Anywhere along Beechwood Blvd in Point Breeze or Squirrel Hill.

Riverview Park Bike Lane

Along Riverview Drive, Riverview Park

Riverview Park is perched on the side of one of the North Hills, overlooking the Ohio River. Riverview Dr is a paved 2.1-mile loop road that includes a bicycle lane. Picnic groves are perched not far from the road wherever they can find a toehold. The bike lane is popular with pedestrians and joggers. However, the loop road is wide and one-way. Since this isn't a through route, traffic is slow and there's plenty of room to pass.

The trail is on the hillside, so it's far from flat. From the entrance near Allegheny Observatory, it runs downhill for a mile to the intersection of Riverview Drive and Woods Run Rd, then back uphill for 1.1 miles to the start. It loses 140 feet of elevation on the way down and regains it coming up.

Rest rooms and drinking water at many picnic groves near the trail. There'a a swimming pool at the top of the hill. Other amenities available not far outside the park.

Access points

Vicinity: Directions begin headed northbound from Pittsburgh on US19, at the corner where US19 turns left from Marshall Av to Perrysville Av about 3 miles north of the West End Bridge.

Trailheads: About a mile north of where US19 turns onto Perrysville Av, turn left on Riverview Av just before the Byzantine Seminary. In a tenth of a mile, turn right on Riverview Dr. Park along Riverview Dr.

North Park Lake Bike Lane

Around North Park Lake, North Park

Bicyclists, joggers, walkers, skaters, baby buggies, dogs, kidcycles, and anything else that moves can be found on this very popular 5-mile loop alongside the road around North Park Lake. The lake forms an irregular "Y", and the trail follows the lake shore. Sometimes it is alongside the lake, sometimes picnic groves lie between the trail and the lake. Aside from the traffic, it's pleasant and scenic. Since this is a loop trail, it has no official ends. People start at any parking area and go either direction.

This is really a bike lane rather than a bike path, as it isn't very well separated from the automobile traffic. For the most part, the paved trail is directly adjacent to the road, separated only by white lines. It's narrow, too—as much as 7' wide, but don't count on more than 6'. Think of this as a 5-mile sidewalk with cross traffic minimized. The adjacent road is fairly busy, too.

Rest rooms and drinking water are available at many picnic groves near the trail. Swim in season at the park wave pool. Other amenities are available not far outside the park.

The Western Pennsylvania Conservancy offers a detailed 2-page description of the trail.

Access points

Vicinity: Directions begin from the intersection of US19 with the Yellow Belt (Ingomar Rd). To reach this point from Pittsburgh, go north on US19 for approximately 10 miles.

Trailheads: From the intersection of US19 and the Yellow Belt (Ingomar Rd), go east on the Yellow Belt for 1.6 miles following signs for North Park. At this point the lake and trail will be on your left. Park at any convenient place around the lake.

Alternate route: You can also reach the trail from PA8. From the intersection of PA8 and the Yellow Belt (here called Wildwood Rd), go west on the Yellow Belt for 2.8 miles to North Park.

South Park Bike Path

Along Corrigan Drive, South Park

A paved path runs 2.2 miles through the park on the east side of Corrigan Drive. Like North Park, this path is popular with walkers, joggers, dog walkers, and everything else. Even on a December weekday it will be busy. In addition to the path, at the north edge of the fairgrounds, a 0.75-mile paved path goes over the hill to the "heart course", a 0.75-mile exercise trail. On the other side of the heart course, a 0.25-mile path returns to Corrigan Drive at McConkey. You can use these to stretch the trip out to a bit over 3 miles.

Rest rooms and drinking water are available at many picnic groves near the trail. Swim in season at the park wave pool. Other amenities are available not far outside the park.

An undeveloped leg of the Montour Trail is only a mile to the south. Unfortunately, there is no good way of getting there.

Access points

Vicinity: Directions begin headed southbound from Pittsburgh on PA88 (Library Rd) about a mile south of the Yellow Belt.

Trailheads: At well-signed Corrigan Dr, turn into South Park. Corrigan Dr runs through the park. Use any handy parking lot.

Trails East and South: Laurel Highlands

Fifty miles east of Pittsburgh, rolling hills rise into the folds of the Appalachian mountains. Although the terrain is rugged, most of the trails here are rail-trails. Like the railroads that preceded them, these trails follow rivers on gentle grades. The major trail system in this region combines the Youghiogheny River and Allegheny Highlands Trails. The route runs upstream along the Youghiogheny River, going southeast from McKeesport to Confluence, then the Casselman River northeast to Rockwood and southeast to Garrett. Eventually it will continue southeast to meet the C&O Canal at Cumberland MD. These trails are now in various stages of development and should be finished by 1998.

Additional trails in the area follow Indian Creek near PA381/711, Linn Run and Summit Rds east of Ligonier, Blacklick Creek near route PA22, and--over on the east side of the ridge--the Frankstown Branch of the Juniata River.

The Pittsburgh to Washington DC Connection

McKeesport PA to Cumberland MD and thence to Washington DC in Allegheny, Westmoreland, Fayette, Somerset Counties PA; Allegany, Washington, Frederick, and Montgomery County MD; and Washington DC

By the turn of the century, it should be possible to ride for over 300 traffic-free miles from near Pittsburgh PA to Washington DC. From Pittsburgh the trail will climb gently along the Youghiogheny River, Casselman River, and Flaugherty Run to the spine of Big Savage Mountain. Here it will cross into Maryland north of Frostburg, then descend to Washington via Jennings Run, Wills Creek and the C&O Canal Towpath along the Potomac River. In Pennsylvania, continuous segments of 20.2, 2.4, 28, and 16.2 miles are now complete, and construction is progressing steadily.

This route between Pittsburgh and Washington DC will involve several distinct trails:

- Allegheny County trails connecting to McKeesport, including Montour, Three Rivers Heritage. and Steel Heritage Trails along the Monongahela River. Distances depend on where you start. Trail organizers are now identifying routes, but none of the current trail development is on this link.
- Northern, or flatwater, section of the Youghiogheny River Trail, 43 miles from McKeesport to Connellsville. In early 1996, 23 miles in 2 sections were finished.
- Southern, or whitewater, section of the Youghiogheny River Trail. The 28-mile trail is complete from Connellsville to Confluence except for a short road link in Ohiopyle.
- Casselman River section of the Allegheny Highlands Trail, 32 miles from Confluence to Meyersdale. As of early 1996, 16.2 miles from Pinkerton to Garrett were complete.

- Flaugherty Run section of the Allegheny Highlands Trail, 11 miles from Meyersdale to the state line. The trail council holds the land, but the Casselman River section will be developed first.
- Maryland section of the Allegheny Highlands Trail, 21 miles across Big Savage Mountain from the state line to Cumberland. 5 miles from Frostburg to the state line is scheduled for 1996 development. Bike lanes on the nearby highway provide a realistic alternative for the connection between Frostburg and Cumberland, except for 1 mile just north of Cumberland ("the narrows").
- C&O Canal Towpath from Cumberland to Washington. This 185-mile trail has been open for many years.

These trails all follow rivers except for the section that crosses Big Savage Mountain. The trail leaves Flaugherty Run near Deal, follows an old railroad grade (with tunnels) along the eastern flank of Big Savage Mountain, and emerges near Frostburg to parallel Jennings Run.

In this guide, we describe each trail in the direction suggested by its mileposts. Unfortunately, this is not consistent: the northern section of the Youghiogheny River trail counts from west to east; the others count from east to west.

When the trail is complete, enough campgrounds will be available for a bicycle camping trip. Assuming that a planned campground near Meyersdale opens, one possibility will take 9 days at a leisurely 35 miles a day:

Day 1	Boston to Adelaide	36 miles
Day 2	Adelaide to Confluence	29 miles
Day 3	Confluence to Meyersdale	32 miles
Day 4	Meyersdale to Evitts Ck Hiker-Biker Camp	37 miles
Day 5	Evitts Ck to Devils Alley Hiker-Biker Camp	36 miles
Day 6	Devils Alley to North Mountain Hiker-Biker Camp	34 miles
Day 7	North Mountain to Killiansburg Cave Hiker-Biker Camp	35 miles
Day 8	Killiansburg Cave to Turtle Run Hiker-Biker Camp	41 miles
Day 9	Turtle Run to Washington DC	34 miles

Assuming that a planned campground at Cedar Creek Park opens, a more ambitious 50-mile/day schedule could take an evening and 6 days:

Evening	Boston to Cedar Creek Park	18 miles
Day 1	Cedar Creek Park to Confluence	47 miles
Day 2	Confluence to Frostburg	48 miles
Day 3	Frostburg to Stickpile Hill Hiker-Biker Camp	51 miles
Day 4	Stickpile Hill to Cumberland Valley Hiker-Biker Camp	54 miles
Day 5	Cumberland Valley to Calico Rocks Hiker-Biker Camp	48 miles
Day 6	Calico Rocks to Washington DC	48 miles

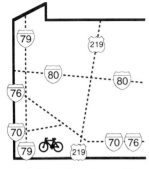

Youghiogheny River Trail

Once trains wound their way up both sides of the Youghiogheny River Gorge en route to the Potomac basin. Now only the CSX (formerly B&O) line on the north side of the river operates. On the south side, a rail-trail connects McKeesport with Confluence on the routes of the former Pittsburgh and Lake Erie (P&LE) and Western Maryland lines.

As of early 1996, three segments were open: 20.2 miles from Boston to Smithton, 2.4 miles from Dickerson Run to Adelaide, and 28 miles from Connellsville to near Confluence. Plans for 1996 include starting the 13.5 miles from Smithton to Dickerson Run (near Dawson), developing a 2-mile spur from Dawson to Linden Hall, finishing the 2.8 miles from Adelaide to Connellsville, and making the final connection between the northern and southern sections of the trail at Connellsville.

Trail organizations

The northern section of the trail is owned and operated by the non-profit Regional Trails Corporation with help from the Southwestern Pa Heritage Preservation Commission. The southern part is developed and managed by Ohiopyle State Park. Three major volunteer organizations support the trail, with participation from a variety of others.

Allegheny County

> Mon/Yough Trail Council
> PO Box 14
> McKeesport PA 15135-0014
> (412) 872-5586

Membership:
> $10/year individual; $15/year family

Fayette County

> Yough River Trail Council
> PO Box 988
> Connellsville PA 15425-0988
> (412) 626-5994

Membership:
> $15/year individual; $25/year family

Ohiopyle State Park

> Ohiopyle State Park
> PO Box 105
> Ohiopyle PA 15470-0105
> (412) 329-8591

Westmoreland County

> Westmoreland Yough Trail Chapter
> PO Box 95, 101 North Water St
> West Newton PA 15089-0095
> (412) 872-5586

Membership:
> $15/year individual; $25/year family

Operations, Boston to Bruner Run

> Regional Trails Corporation
> PO Box 95, 101 North Water St
> West Newton PA 15089-0095
> (412) 872-5586

Membership:
> $25/year individual

Hotline for trail problems

> (412) 872-5586
> In the evenings, this number also takes voicemail for each of the councils

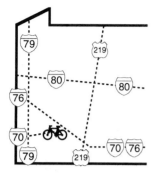

Youghiogheny River Trail, Northern Section

McKeesport to Connellsville, in Allegheny, Westmoreland, and Fayette Counties

The trail will eventually begin in McKeesport's proposed McKee Point Park on the east side of the Youghiogheny River at its confluence with the Monongahela River. This is Pittsburgh and Lake Erie (P&LE) milepost 15; if milepost 0 existed, it would be under the Smithfield St Bridge in Pittsburgh. The trail is planned to run through McKeesport Riverfront Park, cross to the west side of the Yough at the 15th St bridge, and remain on the south side all the way to Confluence. Volunteer trail monitors carry first-aid kits, basic tools, and cellular telephones. Flag one down if you need assistance or have questions.

For now, however, the trail begins at the Boston Riverfront Park (mile 19.1). From here it runs along the edge of Boston, with light industry on the river side and residential back yards on the land side. The warehouse at mile 20.8 has doors to match boxcars on an adjacent siding. The scrap yard at mile 21.2 has three large bells hiding in the shrubbery. Wildflowers proliferate along the shoulders. After fifteen road crossings, including four in the residential area of Greenock (mile 21.3-21.6), the trail leaves civilization and runs along the river in splendid isolation for 5 miles to Buena Vista. In early May trillium carpet the slopes of the 300-foot hillside near miles 22-23. The trail emerges on the flats in a curve of the river and passes the site of the Dravo Methodist Church (mile 24.9). This church, which was founded in 1801. was the oldest in the area until it was destroyed by fire; the cemetery remains. Half a mile past Dravo Cemetery is the ghost town of Stringtown, marked only by a few inconspicuous foundations. Also near here was Indian Queen Alliquippa's summer village.

The trail enters Buena Vista at the Dapul Company (mile 26.4). A picnic pavilion (mile 26.6) greets you in Buena Vista, not far from the swimming pool. For the next 4.8 miles, the trail passes frequently through small towns, alternating between woods and residential communities. In Industry (mile 27.5), note the stained glass windows in the Merritt Primitive Methodist Church. As you pass through Industry, Blythedale (mile 29), and later Smithdale (mile 30), notice the uniform basic shape of the houses—a sign of company towns—and the way subsequent owners have individualized them. The trail emerges on SR2017 at mile 29.5, next to the bridge to Sutersville.

From Sutersville, the trail runs half a mile between the cliff and the river to Smithdale (mile 30). Smithdale is one of several company towns along the trail; it's a particularly good example of how a production-line town can be remodeled into a community of homes with quite distinct personalities. After leaving Smithdale, the trail returns to the bench along the cliff to pass into Westmoreland County at mile 31.4. It emerges in a residential area of Collinsburg (mile 32.3), which blends into West Newton (mile 33.2). You'll see some fine old homes in West Newton just before reaching a major trailhead at PA136. There are stores across the Youghiogheny River, across the PA136 bridge. Be careful at the PA136 intersection; there's a lot of traffic but no signal. At West Newton, the trail leaves civilization for most of a mile, until Buddtown (mile 34), where the trail council's combine car—part passenger, part baggage—sits beside the trail (mile 34.1). Just after leaving Buddtown you pass the remnants of the Banning #4 coal mine and coal cleaning plant (mile 34.5, private property). The mine is closed, but the water treatment plant still runs. Note the cattails across from the water treatment plant.

Then the cliff approaches the river and the trail runs on a wide flat bench between the cliff and the river. A wooden bridge marks the entry to the Manderino Riverfront section of Cedar Creek Park (mile 36.5), where you'll find heat in the restrooms and snacks in restored Cedar Creek Station. The trail continues through the waterfront section of the park to the access road (mile 37.1), then re-enters the woods between the cliff and the river for another mile to Smithton (mile 39.3). Across the river at Smithton you can see the Jones Brewing Company, built in 1907 as the home of Stoney's beer.

Youghiogheny River Trail, Northern Section	
Location	South Versailles and Elizabeth Townships, Allegheny County; Rostraver Township, Westmoreland County; Perry, Franklin, and Dunbar Townships, Fayette County
Trailheads	McKeesport, Boston, West Newton, Cedar Creek Park, Smithton, Dawson, Connellsville
Length, Surface	43 miles planned; 20.2 miles complete Boston-Smithton; 2.4 miles complete Dawson/Dickerson Run-Adelaide
Character	Busy to uncrowded, wooded, shady, flat
Usage restrictions	Horses ok beside trail—stay off improved surface; no motorized vehicles; no snowmobiles
Amenities	Rest rooms, water ,bike renal, food, swimming
Driving time from Pittsburgh	45 minutes to 1 hour 30 minutes

For about 14.5 miles from Smithton (mile 39.3) to the Dickerson Run yard (mile 52.8) across the river from Dawson, the trail is unimproved. This section of the trail continues along the Youghiogheny River through old company towns and their mines. The surface varies from hardpack to rough double-track, but it's passable for mountain bikes. You can use parallel, low-traffic roads in Van Meter (mile 40.1 to 41.2) and Whitsett (mile 42.7 to 44.5) to avoid some of the rough track. Van Meter (mile 40.5) served the Darr Mine, whose coal cleaning plant you'll see at mile 41.4. Van Meter became a virtual ghost town almost overnight in December 1907, when disasters in both the Naomi and Darr Mines claimed first 34, then 239 lives. Under the Norfolk and Western High Bridge (mile 42), watch out for a sharp ditch across the trail. The Banning #2 mine (office at Whitsett Rd, mile 42.7) was served by Whitsett (mile 43). The large red house on the road near the river (mile 43) was built by Ralph Whitsett Sr., the town founder.

For the last part of the unimproved section, from Layton (mile 45.7) to Dawson/Dickerson Run (mile 52.8), there is no road access, and the area has a considerable history of 4WD and pickup traffic. The trail developers are now attempting to discourage this, but the vehicle traffic has left a legacy of rough, semi-packed tracks. You'll pass the remains of a brick factory and its associated kilns (mile 46.2) and cross several small streams with dubious (i.e., unsafe) bridges.

Dickerson Run (mile 52.8), across the river from Dawson, was once a major switching yard. The P&LE operated the 2500-car yard under a joint switching agreement with the Western Maryland RR from 1912 to 1970. It will eventually provide a large parking lot and trailhead. For 2.5 miles south from here, to Adelaide (mile 55.2), the trail again runs close to the river, finished in crushed limestone. This area was once known as the coke capital of the world. Hundreds of coke ovens in one or two rows dot the hillsides just above the trail. An interpretive sign at mile 54 describes their history.

Dravo Cemetery, mile 24.9

At Adelaide (mile 55.2) the trail reverts to double-tracked packed cinders with some loose coarse gravel. It was closed in 1995 to strip-mine coal under the trail, with profits supporting trail development. It should be completed to Connellsville (mile 58) in early 1996. A ramp will wind down the hill to Yough River Park near the William Crawford cabin. Here it will connect with the bike path that carries the trail along 3rd St through Connellsville to the southern section of the trail. At Connellsville the river leaves the farm and mining lands in the valley and enters the water gap through Chestnut Ridge. As you cross to the southern section, the character of the trail changes from flatwater to whitewater, and the setting changes from rural mining towns to near-wilderness gorge.

Local history, attractions

The railroad that once ran here opened for business as the Pittsburgh, McKeesport, & Youghiogheny Railroad—PMc&Y, also known as the "P-Mickey"—in October 12, 1883. Almost immediately, on January 1, 1884, it became part of the Pittsburgh and Lake Erie Railroad (P&LERR). In 1887 it became a New York Central (NYC) line, which merged with the Pennsy in the 1960s to become the Penn Central. The collapse of the Penn Central made the P&LE independent again in 1978. P&LE filed to abandon the line in 1990, after the decline of the coal industry reduced traffic too much. Most of the P&LE's business was related to steel-making: coal, ore, coke, and limestone. P&LE boxcars bore the slogan "Serves the Steel Centers."

Industrial activity in the valley revolved around the steel industry, and the trail shows conspicuous remnants of both steel and mining activity. The landscape in some areas is dominated by piles of mine tailings (also called gob, or red-dog). Several ruins of coal-processing plants remain. Less obvious, but still visible, are a number of areas of mine drainage. Spot these by the bright orange soil under the waterfall or creek. Remains of coke ovens lie near the trail at several locations. Several of the towns along the trail are former company towns.

A short-lived canal served the Youghiogheny River between West Newton and McKeesport. The Youghiogheny Navigation Company built two dams with locks to overcome a 27-foot change in elevation and create a slackwater navigation system. The canal began operations in 1850 but was destroyed by a flood in January 1865.

Coke oven, near mile 54

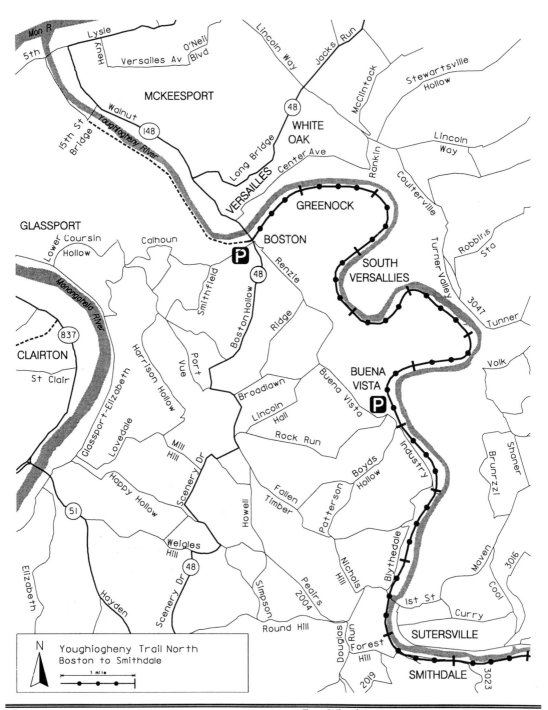

Youghiogheny Trail North
Boston to Smithdale

N

1 mile

Free-Wheeling Easy in Western Pennsylvania

Development plans

The trail between Adelaide and Yough River Park in Connellsville is scheduled for completion by early summer 1996. The major missing link, 14 miles from Smithton Beach to the Dickerson Run RR yard across the river from Dawson, is scheduled to start development in 1996. Funding is largely in place and plans have been approved.

Linden Hall is planning to develop a 2-mile spur connecting to the trail at Dawson by summer 1996. They will add a mountain biking area at Linden Hall sometime later.

The extension from Boston to McKeesport (mile 19.1 to mile 15) has reached the engineering stages.

The trail organizations hold regular volunteer trail development activities on most Saturdays with decent weather. Several Boy Scouts have improved the trail through their Eagle Scout projects. These projects include restoration of mileposts, interpretive displays, and environmental work.

In addition to completing the trail, plans call for development of river access areas for fishing and boating. Historic sites will be preserved and developed. Overnight facilities for through travelers will include B&Bs, hostels, and primitive campsites at four locations along the trail.

Access points

Vicinity: Directions begin headed southeast on PA51 at Elizabeth, where PA51 crosses the Monongahela River. To reach this point from Pittsburgh, pick up PA51 anywhere in the South Hills and turn south or southeast.

Boston trailhead: Go southeast on PA51 from the Monongahela River for about 4 miles to PA48 near Round Hill Regional Park. Turn north on PA48, and follow its twists and turns for 6-8 miles to a 5-way intersection in Boston, just before you cross the Youghiogheny River. At this point (the south end of Boston Bridge), turn west (left), then immediately back north (right, toward the river). In less than a block, the road crosses the trail, and there is plenty of parking at this point. If you go a bit farther, you'll come to a PA Fish Commission boat ramp. *Alternate route:* If you're coming from the east side of Pittsburgh, it's quicker to reach Boston via PA48 south from the Parkway and US30.

West Newton trailhead: Go southeast on PA51 from the Monongahela River for about 6 miles to PA136. Turn east (left) on PA136 and continue about 5 miles into the outskirts of West Newton. Just before crossing the Youghiogheny River, turn south (right) into the parking area at the west end of the PA136 bridge. There's additional parking on the north side of PA136, along Collinsburg Rd.

Cedar Creek trailhead: go southeast on PA51 from the Monongahela River for about 9 miles and follow signs to the Park. In quick succession you'll turn left on Concord Lane, left on Lynn Rd, and right on Port Royal Rd. Just after passing Timm's Lane, turn left at the main entrance to Cedar Creek Park. Follow this road downhill until it reaches the

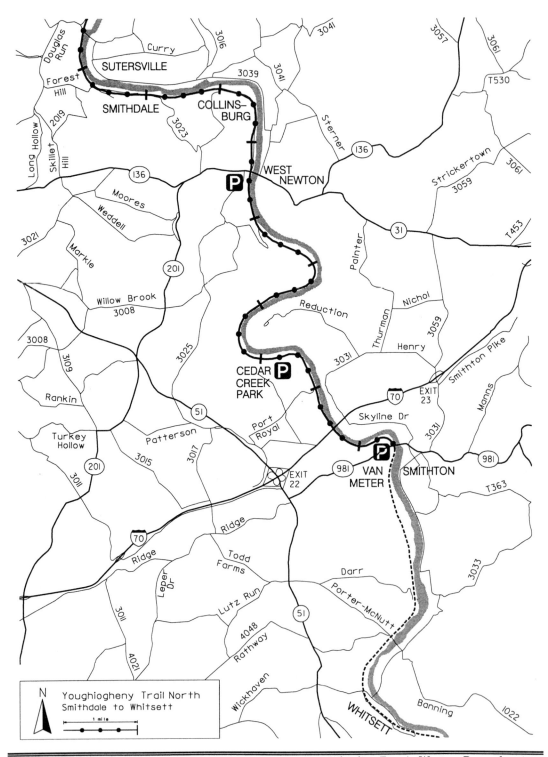

Youghiogheny Trail North
Smithdale to Whitsett

N

1 mile

Free-Wheeling Easy in Western Pennsylvania

flood plain. There's one parking lot just before you cross the trail and several more a little farther along the road.

Smithton trailhead: Go southeast on PA51 from the Monongahela River for about 9-10 miles. Just after passing I70, turn east (left) on PA981 toward Smithton. Follow PA981 for 1.5 miles, to a point just before crossing the Youghiogheny River (the west end of the PA981 bridge). Immediately before the bridge's guard rail starts, turn down a short road that leads sharply down to the parking area near the river.

Dawson/Dickerson Run trailhead: Go southeast on PA51 from the Monongahela River for about 18 miles to the PA201 interchange for Vanderbilt and Dawson. (Note: this will be the second intersection of PA51 and PA201; watch your mileage and don't be fooled.) Take PA201 east toward Vanderbilt and Connellsville. In Vanderbilt, turn north (left) on PA819 and follow it downhill almost to the Youghiogheny River. As you come to the Dawson-Liberty Bridge, turn left (northwest) just at the end of the bridge. Almost immediately turn left down a ramp, making a 180-degree descending left turn. This now ends at a barrier with little parking, but there should eventually be a parking lot near the trail. This brings you to a gate; there will eventually be a trailhead parking lot here. For now, look for parking on the road nearby.

Connellsville trailhead: Go southeast on PA51 from the Monongahela River for about 18 miles to the PA201 interchange for Vanderbilt and Dawson. (Note: this will be the second intersection of PA51 and PA201; watch your mileage and don't be fooled.) Take PA201 east toward Vanderbilt and Connellsville. Just before the intersection with PA711 and US119, turn north (left) into the vast cindered area between the southbound lanes of US119 and the termination of PA201. Go back beyond the produce stand and the caboose to where the cable closes off the area. This is trailhead parking. The northern section of the trail takes off on the other side of the gate, past the restored yard office. When the trail to Yough River Park is finished in 1996, you'll also be able to park near there.

Other trailheads: There are additional trailheads at Buena Vista, Cedar Creek Park, Sutersville, and Adelaide (fee parking at campground). These are reached by various back roads. Take a good map with you.

Amenities

Rest rooms, water: Seasonal portable toilets at Boston, West Newton, and Smithton trailheads and at ballfields in Greenock, Industry, and Blythedale. Rest rooms at Cedar Creek Park all year, at Yough River Park (may be closed in winter), and eventually at the restored yard office near mile 58. Drinking water at playground in Industry, in Cedar Creek Park, and at River's Edge Campground in Adelaide.

Bike shop, rental: Bike shops with rentals at R&R Bicycles in Boston, West Newton Cycles in West Newton (half a block from the trail), and Bikes Unlimited (at the "rail-trail traffic light") or Col. Crawford in Connellsville. Rentals at Smitty's in Boston (mile 19.8), at the restored train station in Cedar Creek Park (mile 36.7), and at Adelaide Campground (mile 55.1, just a few).

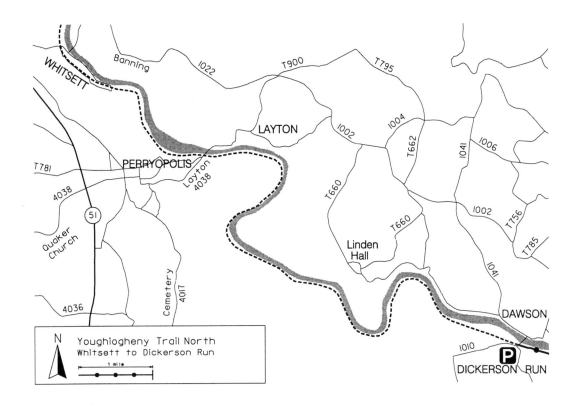

N

Youghiogheny Trail North
Whitsett to Dickerson Run

1 mile

Restaurant, groceries: Boston has a Foodland grocery store near Boston Bridge and Boston Diner, three blocks toward Greenock. There are several other restaurants in Boston and just across Boston Bridge; the church sometimes serves dinner, too. Near the trail at mile 19.8, Smitty's Yough River Park offers riverside meals. Three blocks from the pavilion at Buena Vista, the Volunteer Fire Department operates a seasonal snack bar next to the swimming pool. Just south of Buena Vista, near mile 27.0, Valle[y] Market has groceries and a deli counter. Sutersville, across the Yough at mile 29.5, has restaurants. A dairy stand half a block from the Sutersville trailhead offers ice cream and sandwiches. Half a block from the West Newton trailhead a Rite-Aid offers snacks and light groceries. West Newton, across the river at mile 33.2, has a Giant Eagle 0.7 miles north of the bridge plus several restaurants, including a Dairy-Land on N Water St near the Giant Eagle, Fay's Restaurant on S 2nd St half a block south of PA136, and several pizza shops. At Layton (mile 45.3), snacks are seasonally available at Hazelbaker Canoe livery, across the river and a quarter mile up the road. Dawson (across the river, at mile 52.8) has groceries, snacks, and a restaurant. The campground at Adelaide (mile 55.1) has a small store with groceries, snacks, and some fast food. In Connellsville, a Sheetz market is just across the PA711/US119 intersection from the trailhead. Soft drink or juice vending machines have been installed at Dapul Company (mile 26.4), Valle[y] Dairy (mile 27.0), and the old company store in Van Meter (mile 40.8).

Camping, simple lodging: River's Edge Campground lies along the trail near Adelaide; they offer a discount to campers who hike or bike in. Campgrounds are planned near Buena Vista, Cedar Creek County Park, Layton, and Connellsville. *Trail Book '95* contains ads for Bed-and-Breakfasts close to the trail at Buena Vista (1 mile up the hill) and Dawson.

Swimming, fishing: Pools at Buena Vista and River's Edge Campground (both fee). The Youghiogheny may look enticing for unsupervised swimming, but it carries a considerable amount of raw sewage. Exercise caution, especially if the water is high. Swimming is prohibited at the Fish Commission access at Boston and at Cedar Creek Park. Signs at Connellsville Riverfront Park remind you that the park was not created to entice swimming and you do so at your own risk. Fishing is good to excellent all along the trail. Common catches are trout and small-mouth bass plus other varieties including catfish. The Yough is stocked with trout at West Newton. Record-size bass have been caught near Smithton. We see fisherfolk all along the river; one day we met a fisherman with a 35" muskie.

Winter sports: Cross-country skiing. No snowmobiles.

Maps, guides, other references

Trail Book '95: A Users Guide to the Youghiogheny River Trail and the Allegheny Highlands Trail. Available from the trail councils and many local businesses.

Tim Palmer. *Youghiogheny, Appalachian River.* University of Pittsburgh Press, 1984.

USGS Topographic Maps: McKeesport, Donora, Smithton, Fayette City, Dawson, Connellsville.

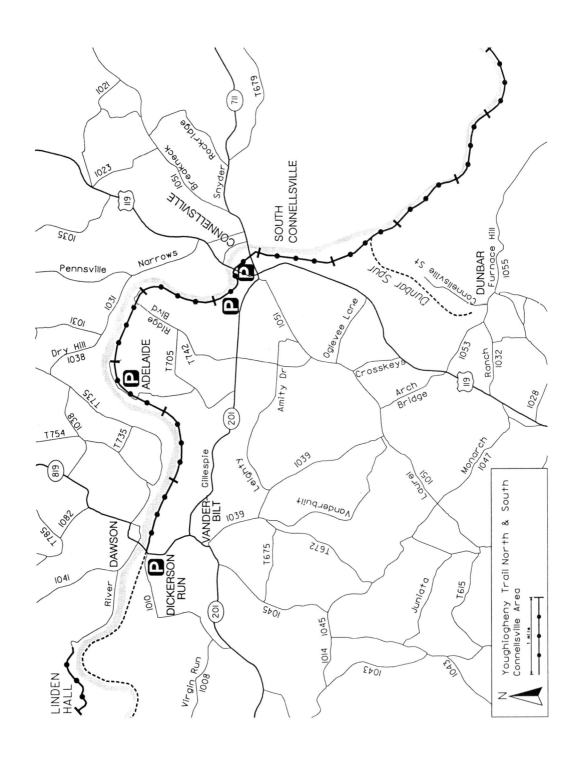

Free-Wheeling Easy in Western Pennsylvania

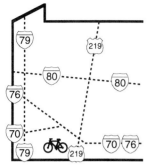

Youghiogheny River Trail, Southern Section

Confluence to Connellsville, in Fayette County

George Washington followed the Youghiogheny to Ohiopyle in 1754 in his search for a water route to Fort Duquesne (now Pittsburgh), but he gave up when he encountered the falls and rapids below. Modern visitors cycle this route through the Appalachians on the former route of the Western Maryland Railroad.

This trail has been named as one of the best walking trails in the world. Writing in the October 1994 issue of *Travel and Leisure Magazine*, Rita Ariyoshi named the Youghiogheny River Trail among 19 paths from France to New Zealand as "The World's Best Walks". It's a popular trail, and hence can be a busy one. In nine years from 1986 to 1995 the number of user-days grew from 45,000 to 200,000.

The zero milepost of the trail is at the PA281 bridge over the Youghiogheny River in Confluence; the trail runs northwest from here toward Connellsville. For about 0.6 miles the trail goes downstream on Ramcat Hollow Rd to a right turn onto the trail, which is finished in crushed limestone. From here to Ohiopyle, the trail is isolated. The river is frequently visible, and you can enjoy watching the canoeists in the easy rapids between Victoria and Ohiopyle. Along this portion of the trail you'll see remnants of the railroad, most notably cuts through hills such as the one at mile 2.5, fills that kept the railbed nearly level over hollows such as the one at mile 2.7, and retaining walls like the one at mile 5.7. You'll also see traces of old farms, such as the fruit trees in the field at mile 6.3 and the long stacked fieldstone fence that runs from mile 6.5 to mile 6.7. Half a dozen or so benches along the trail provide chances to rest and watch the traffic go by.

At mile 9.8 the trail enters the Ohiopyle parking lot. A restored railroad station at mile 10.1 hosts the information center. Ohiopyle is a popular tourist area and has bike rental facilities. The trail is likely to be very busy with both pedestrians and bicyclists in the vicinity of Ohiopyle. From the information center the trail follows roads across the Youghiogheny River (be alert to automobile traffic) and into the parking area for the Ferncliff Natural Area, a wildflower preserve. Signs at the end of the parking area direct you back onto the trail at mile 10.4. A right in the parking area takes you to the American Youth Hostel. Although it's only half a mile across Ferncliff peninsula before you cross the river again, the river takes 2 miles to go around the peninsula, dropping 80 ft in the process.

As the trail leaves Ohiopyle it crosses the Youghiogheny River on a converted trestle. Notice how much farther above the river you are here than in Ohiopyle. This trestle is a good place to watch raft trips negotiate (or fail to) Railroad Rapid just upstream. From Ohiopyle to Bruner Run (mile 16) the trail runs well above the river, and the woods are too thick for good views of the rafting and kayaking action. However, you'll hear, if not see, the rafting crowds; signposts with cryptic 2-letter abbreviations mark paths down the steep hill to some of the named rapids. You can also enjoy the maturing deciduous forest, the cascading feeder streams, and the June display of laurel and rhododendron. Note especially the rock face with coal seams at mile 13.7 and the railroad ties remaining alongside the trail at mile 15. Half a dozen benches provide resting places. Several hiking trails intersect our trail: Great Gorge at mile 10.6, Beech at mile 10.7, Jonathan Run at mile 13.5, and Kentuck at miles 13.5 and 13.7. Bicycles are forbidden on most, if not all, of these, but the trail to the campground is an exception. The trail gradient is more noticeable between Ohiopyle and Bruner Run than elsewhere (not surprisingly, as that's also the more difficult whitewater section). Bruner Run is the termination of the very popular whitewater trip that begins at Ohiopyle.

Youghiogheny River Trail, Southern Section	
Location	Confluence to Ohiopyle to Connellsville, Henry Clay and Stewart Townships, Fayette Counties
Trailheads	Confluence, Ohiopyle, Connellsville
Surface	28 miles, crushed limestone
Character	Busy to crowded, wooded, mostly shady, flat to gentle grade
Usage restrictions	No motorized vehicles; no snowmobiles; no horses
Amenities	Rest rooms, water, bike rental, food, wading, fishing
Driving time from Pittsburgh	1 hour 30-45 minutes southeast to Ohiopyle; 1 hour 15 minutes southeast to Connellsville

From Bruner Run for about 8 miles to Wheeler Bottom (mile 24.7), the trail is isolated in the Youghiogheny gorge. A spectacular view opens at mile 16.9, where a huge cement wall holds up the hillside at a pipeline crossing. The solitude is interrupted only at mile 19.4 by Camp Carmel, a small church camp that is rarely occupied. At mile 25, just before crossing the first trestle, you pass an unfinished cinder path along Dunbar Creek that will eventually become the Dunbar spur. For now, stay on the finished trail and cross the first of two high trestles that take you into Connellsville.

In Connellsville the trail emerges behind the former Connellsville Sportswear plant on First St (mile 27). It moves over to Third St in a bike lane separated from auto traffic by landscaped planters. The trail follows Third St through mixed residential and commercial areas of Connellsville to parking near Yough Riverfront Park, about 28 miles from Confluence. The crossing of busy PA711 is protected by a traffic signal. At Connellsville the river leaves the water gap through Chestnut Ridge and enters the farm and mining lands in the valley. Here you cross to the northern section of the trail, the character of the trail changes from whitewater to flatwater, and the setting changes from near-wilderness gorge to rural mining towns. In 1996 this section of the trail should connect with the northern section at Riverfront Park.

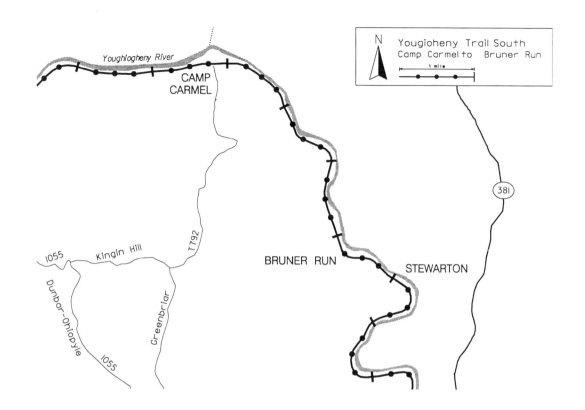

Local history, attractions

Monongahela Indians lived in the basin between 900 and 1600 AD. After they left, Delaware, Shawnee, and Iroquois Indians used the area as a hunting ground. Old records indicate that the name Ohiopyle was derived from the Indian word "Ohiopehhle", which means "white frothy water", a reference to the large falls on the Youghiogheny River. If you find the spelling of these names daunting, take heart: The river was called Yok-yo-gane in its first appearance on a map, in 1737. Since then it has been called Yawyawganey (1751), Joxhio Geni and Yoxhio Geni (1755), Yehiogany (1784), and even Yuh-wiac-hanne (early land grant).

In the 19th century, the falls made Ohiopyle a commercial center. Water power supported variously a sawmill, a gristmill, a planing mill, and an electric power plant. After the Western Maryland Railroad arrived in 1914, Ohiopyle became a popular resort destination. Round trip fare from Pittsburgh was $1.00.

In years past, two railroads used the Youghiogheny valley to pass through Laurel and Chestnut Ridges—the Baltimore and Ohio on the north bank, and the Western Maryland on the south bank. The B&O merged with the Chesapeake and Ohio and the Western Maryland to become part of CSX. The B&O tracks are still in use, now as part of CSX on Conrail tracks, but the Western Maryland tracks were abandoned in the 1970's.

River view, mile 16.9

Now Ohiopyle relies primarily on tourism. The State Park offers 19,000 acres of natural beauty, including the Falls, Ferncliff Natural Area, whitewater rafting and kayaking, and hiking. A 10-mile mountain bike trail (Sugarloaf Snowmobile and Mountain Bike Area) has been established on the southwest side of SR2012 between Ohiopyle and Confluence. Only roads connect the mountain bike area and the river trail.

Development plans

The trail is complete from just north of Confluence to Connellsville except for a short section on roads in Ohiopyle. The road crossing of the Youghiogheny River in Ohiopyle may be eliminated if it's possible to put the trail on the old Western Maryland trestle.

At the Confluence end, less that half a mile separates the current end of the trail from the PA281 bridge across the Youghiogheny River. Some land exchange is required to complete the trail, and a better river crossing is needed to reduce congestion on the bridge. This should be done before the trail is linked with the Allegheny Highlands Trail along the Casselman River. Discussions of these plans are in progress.

Plans also call for a 1.2-mile side spur to Dunbar.

Extension of the trail into Confluence proper and additional rest rooms and parking are also under discussion.

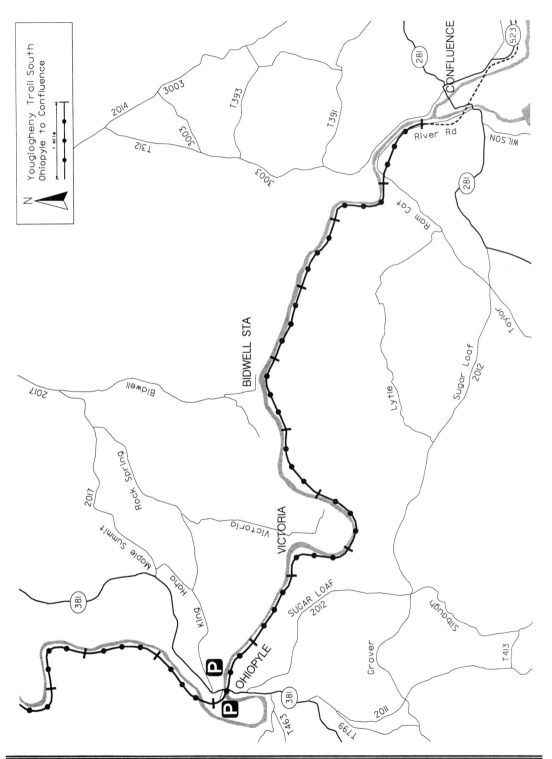

Access points

Vicinity: Access is at Confluence (southern trailhead), Ohiopyle (central trailhead), and Connellsville (northern trailhead).

For Confluence and Ohiopyle, directions begin southbound on PA381 entering Ohiopyle. To reach this point from Pittsburgh take the PA Turnpike (I76) to Donegal. Turn east (left) on PA31. About 2 miles later turn south (right) on PA381. Follow PA381 about 18 miles to Ohiopyle.

For Connellsville, directions begin at the intersection of PA711 and US119 in Connellsville. To reach this point from Pittsburgh take the PA Turnpike (I76) to New Stanton. Follow signs to go south on US119 about 16 miles to Connellsville.

Southern trailhead (Confluence): Follow PA381 through most of Ohiopyle and turn southeast (left) on SR2012 at the Boater's Change house. Go 8.1 miles to PA281 and turn north on PA281. When PA281 turns right to cross the Youghiogheny River, you may either continue straight on River Rd to trailhead parking at Ramcat Hollow or else follow PA281 across the bridge to park in Confluence and ride back across this bridge. *Alternate route:* For a shortcut to Ramcat Hollow trailhead, turn left off SR2012 onto Ram Cat Rd 7.3 miles from Ohiopyle.

Central trailhead (Ohiopyle): As PA381 enters Ohiopyle, it crosses an active rail line, then the Youghiogheny River. A right turn just before the bridge takes you to the Ferncliff parking lot, access for the Ohiopyle-Bruner Run section. The first left turn after crossing the river takes you past the old train station to parking for the Ohiopyle-Confluence section.

Northern trailhead (Connellsville): From the traffic light at the intersection of PA711 and US119 in Connellsville, go north on PA711 for a few blocks to Third St. You'll recognize it by the traffic light, the bike shop, and the separate bike lane. Turn left on Third St and follow the bicycle trail to trail parking.

Amenities

Rest rooms, water: Rest rooms and water at Confluence and Ohiopyle trailheads.

Bike shop, rentals: Bike shops and rentals in Ohiopyle, Connellsville, and Confluence.

Restaurant, groceries: Groceries and restaurants in Connellsville, Ohiopyle and Confluence. River's Edge Cafe in Confluence is popular.

Camping, simple lodging: Camping at Outflow Campground, at the base of Youghiogheny Dam, near Confluence. There's also a campground at Ohiopyle State Park high on the ridge above the trail. You wouldn't want to ride up the steep, narrow, busy road, but the State Park advises us that you can take bikes up the trail marked "To Campground" at the north end of the bridge at mile 10.6. In Ohiopyle, American Youth Hostel on Ferncliff Peninsula and Falls Market in town.

Wheeler Bottom Trestle, mile 25

Swimming, fishing: The State Park does not allow swimming (to do so would require lifeguards). Wading is permitted, however. Be careful of the current in the Youghiogheny River. The north side of the river at Ferncliff is popular. If you enter the water near Confluence, be aware that the water is probably freshly released from the bottom of Youghiogheny Lake and hence quite cold, even in summer. Fishing is good to excellent all along the trail, in part because it's cool all summer. Common catches are trout and small-mouth bass plus other varieties including catfish.

Winter sports: Cross-country skiing. No snowmobiles.

Maps, guides, other references

Trail Book '95: A Users Guide to the Youghiogheny River Trail and the Allegheny Highlands Trail. Available from the trail councils and many local businesses.

Ohiopyle State Park information brochure.

Tim Palmer. *Youghiogheny, Appalachian River.* University of Pittsburgh Press, 1984.

USGS Topographic Maps: Confluence, Ohiopyle, Mill Run, South Connellsville, Connellsville.

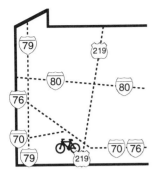

Allegheny Highlands Trail

Cumberland MD to Frostburg MD, over Big Savage Mountain into PA, then along Casselman River to Confluence in Somerset County PA

The Allegheny Highlands trail will run for 62 miles through woods and small towns, climbing from the terminus of the C&O Canal Towpath at Cumberland MD along Wills Creek and Jennings Run to Frostburg MD, then up the eastern flank of Big Savage Mountain. After crossing under the crest of the mountain in a kilometer-long tunnel, it will descend along Flaugherty Run to the Casselman River at Meyersdale PA, then follow the Casselman to Confluence.

Initial development is concentrating on the Casselman River section. The continuation along Flaugherty Run will follow. The exact routing of the Maryland section is now being negotiated. Since the sections of this trail that are not officially open are officially closed to the public, we give only short descriptions of the future routes.

Allegheny Highlands Trail, Maryland Section

From Cumberland to Frostburg, then along Big Savage Mountain to Maryland state line in Allegany County MD

The Maryland Department of Natural Resources is planning to develop the trail from Cumberland to the Maryland/Pennsylvania state line. They hope to share the right-of-way of the Western Maryland Scenic Railroad for 15 miles to Frostburg, then use the right-of-way of the former Western Maryland RR for 5 miles north to the Mason-Dixon line. They are also considering a 7-mile side trail to the town of Mt Savage.

The wildest, most remote part of the trail lies in western Maryland. Here you find rugged mountains, hardwood forest, high wooded ridges, and narrow stream valleys. The parallel ridges and valleys run from northeast to southwest, and over 55% of the land in the county is on slopes greater than 25%. Nevertheless, the grade on the right of way is less than 3%. Since the trail will traverse mountainous sideslopes, the views will be spectacular. Unsurprisingly, the trail winds 20 miles to cover the 9-mile straight-line distance from Cumberland northwest to the PA connection on Savage mountain.

When this section of trail is completed, it will provide unique glimpses into western Maryland's prehistoric and early industrial past. In Cumberland, the trail will connect with the C&O Canal Towpath at the Western Maryland RR station, which also serves as the eastern terminus of the Western Maryland Scenic RR. From Cumberland, the trail will arch northwest, then southwest to Frostburg. The trailhead at Frostburg will be the Cumberland and Pennsylvania RR Depot. Built in 1891, it is also the western terminus of the Western Maryland Scenic RR. From Frostburg the trail will climb the flank of Big Savage Mountain to join the Pennsylvania section of the trail.

The trail will feature two unique natural areas: the Bone Cave and the Narrows. The Cumberland Bone Cave is a limestone cave recognized as one of the most significant deposits of Pleistocene animal remains in the eastern US. About 4 miles northwest of Cumberland, it was discovered during railroad construction in 1912. Excavation yielded fossils of 46 animal species, 28 of which are extinct. The Cumberland Narrows is the mile-long gorge of Wills Creek, 1.5 miles northwest of Cumberland. The highway, the creek, a CSX railroad line, and the scenic railroad all squeeze through this spectacular slot between Haystack and Wills Mountains.

Trail organization

Trail Manager for Allegheny Highlands Trail (Maryland Section)

Maryland Department of Natural Resources
Public Lands and Forestry
Greenways and Resource Planning
580 Taylor Av, D-3
Annapolis, MD 21401

(410) 974-3654

Allegheny Highlands Trail, Flaugherty Run Section

Along Flaugherty Run from Maryland state line near Deal to Meyersdale in Somerset County

From the Mason-Dixon Line, the trail will continue for 11 miles on the Western Maryland route to Meyersdale. The major development challenge will be the kilometer-long Big Savage Tunnel, which takes the trail under the mountain and saves 200 feet of climb. Emerging from the woods at Deal, it will descend along Flaugherty Run to Meyersdale.

Until the trail is complete, a decent alternative from Deal to Meyersdale is SR2006. There's no really good alternative from Deal to Cumberland. The direct route uses SR2011 to get from Deal to PA160 and follows PA160 (narrow winding road with traffic, alas), which becomes MD47, to MD36 to Cumberland.

Trail organization

Trail Manager for Allegheny Highlands Trail (Flaugherty Run Section)

Hank Parke
Somerset County Rails to Trails Association
829 North Center Av
Somerset PA 15501-1029

(814) 445-6431

Membership: $20/year individual or family

Allegheny Highlands Trail, Casselman Section

Along Casselman River from Meyersdale to Confluence in Somerset County

The completed trail will follow the Casselman River for 31 miles from Meyersdale to Confluence, where it will connect with the Youghiogheny River Trail. In fall of 1995, the 7 mile section from Rockwood to Garrett and the 7.5-mile section from Rockwood through Markleton to the trestle before Pinkerton Tunnel were complete. This provides a continuous 16.2-mile section, from mile 16.5 nearly to mile 33 of the final trail.

The surface is packed limestone, a generous 11-12 feet wide with an additional foot or two of ballast on the shoulder. Several benches beside the trail offer a chance to admire the scenery. The trail is generally 20-40 feet above the Casselman River, affording views of the moderate rapids and, in season, of canoeists and kayakers. During early spring snowmelt, waterfalls and creeks cascade over the adjacent cliffs and out of the hollows.

At Garrett, the trail begins near the waterworks (mile 16.3). From here to Rockwood, little intrudes on the woods and river. At mile 18.5, a fine rock cliff forms the side of the trail. Across the river, five rectangular openings mark the location of an old mine. The gob heap that appears at mile 22.8 signals that you're approaching Rockwood.

The trail drops from the railroad grade to cross the road at Rockwood (mile 23.3). A large parking lot provides the most convenient access from the PA Turnpike.

Past the parking lot, the trail passes the remnants of a mining complex and coal tipple (mile 23.7). At mile 24.2 a bench provides a perch from which to watch the cascade leaping off the cliff, and at mile 24.8 another stream emerges in a wooden trough. The trail continues in woods to mile 26.5, where the town of Casselman comes into view across the river. Just north of milepost 27 (which is out of place, at mile 27.14), a waterfall gurgles gently down the cliff face.

Allegheny Highlands Trail, Casselman Section	
Location	Addison, Lower Turkeyfoot, Upper Turkeyfoot, Black, Summit Twps, Somerset County
Trailheads	Markleton, Rockwood, Garrett,
Length, Surface	16.2 miles developed, crushed limestone
Character	Uncrowded, wooded, mixed sun and shade, flat
Usage restrictions	No motorized vehicles; no snowmobiles
Amenities	Portable toilets, bike rentals, food
Driving time from Pittsburgh	1 hour 45 minutes southeast

At mile 29.4 the trail drops again to the parking area and road crossing at Markleton. Another 1.7 miles brings you to the trestle across the Casselman River at the Pinkerton Horn (mile 31.1). The outstanding feature of the trail lies just ahead, to the southwest: the 850-foot Pinkerton Tunnel, dated 1911. Part of the ceiling has fallen in, and

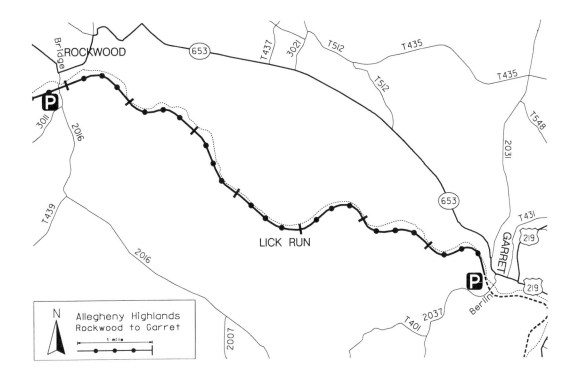

extensive, expensive repairs will be needed before the trail can continue through the tunnel. For now, the trail goes 1.5 miles around Pinkerton Horn on an older railroad grade and meets rejoins the main route at the other end of the tunnel, just before another trestle. The second trestle should be rebuilt and open in early spring 1996. Be careful on this segment: the railbed is narrow and the hillside is steep. The trail is 10' wide, but there are no shoulders. For now, the trail stops at the end of the second trestle.

The spirit of the railroad will be with you on this trail: Full-fidelity sound is provided by the frequent trains of the active Baltimore and Ohio line just across the river.

Development plans

Plans for 1996 call for extending the trail 6 miles from Garrett to Meyersdale. The major feature of this section is the Salisbury Viaduct, a 1900-foot steel trestle up to 100' high that crosses the Casselman River and US219 north of Meyersdale. Restoration of this trestle, including deck and railings, will represent a large part of the project. In anticipation of the extension to Meyersdale, the historical society is restoring the Meyersdale train station.

The trail will also be extended to Confluence, where it will eventually connect with the Youghiogheny River Trail.

Access points

Vicinity: Directions begin at the Somerset exit of the PA Turnpike (I76).

Garrett trailhead: From the Somerset Turnpike exit, go south on US219 about 15 miles to Garrett. Turn right on PA653. Go 0.2 miles to Berlin St and turn left. Go 0.1 miles on Berlin St, turning right just after crossing the bridge. Follow this road 0.3 miles to trailhead parking. *Alternate route:* A shortcut to Garrett uses SR2031 to avoid following US219 all the way east to the town of Berlin and back west. The intersection of SR2031 with PA653 is west of Garrett, so turn left from SR2031 onto PA653, then right on Berlin.

Rockwood trailhead: From the Somerset Turnpike exit, follow signs to go south on PA281 about 10 miles to PA653. Go east on PA653 2.7 miles to Rockwood, where it's also called Bridge St. Where PA653 turns left to avoid crossing the Casselman River, continue straight on Bridge St (SR2016) to cross the river. The entrance to the parking lot is on the right about 25 yards past the bridge. *Alternate route:* A shorter, but more complicated, route to Rockwood follows Coxes Creek: From the Somerset Turnpike exit follow signs to go south on PA281. At the first traffic light after joining PA281, turn left on SR3015. Follow SR3015 8.2 miles to Rockwood. At the stop sign where PA653 enters from the left, go straight on PA653. Follow this road (Main St) for 0.8 miles through Rockwood. When PA653 turns right to leave the river, turn left on Bridge St (SR2016) to cross the river and park as above. Signs in Rockwood direct you to the trail.

Markleton trailhead: From the Somerset Turnpike exit, go south on PA281 about 18 miles to SR3011. Turn left on SR3011 and follow its twists and turns to cross the Casselman River. Just after crossing the river, turn right into the parking lot. This parking area also serves whitewater boaters on the Casselman River.

Amenities

Rest rooms, water: Portable toilets, probably seasonal, at Garrett, Rockwood, and Markleton trailheads. No water.

Bike shop, rentals: Rentals at The Country Trail in Rockwood just across the bridge from the trailhead.

Restaurant, groceries: The Garrett Country Store/BP gas station in Garrett (near the intersection of PA653 and US219). In Rockwood, just across the bridge from the trailhead; also restaurants in Rockwood proper. In Markleton, a juice machine and pop machine at the house between the trail crossing and the river.

Camping, simple lodging: Several bed-and-breakfast inns are being planned along the route. There's one "15 minutes" from Rockwood according to *Trail Guide '94*. The Corps of Engineers operates Outflow Campground at the base of Youghiogheny Dam, about half a mile from Confluence. We also understand that another campground along the trail near Meyersburg is being planned.

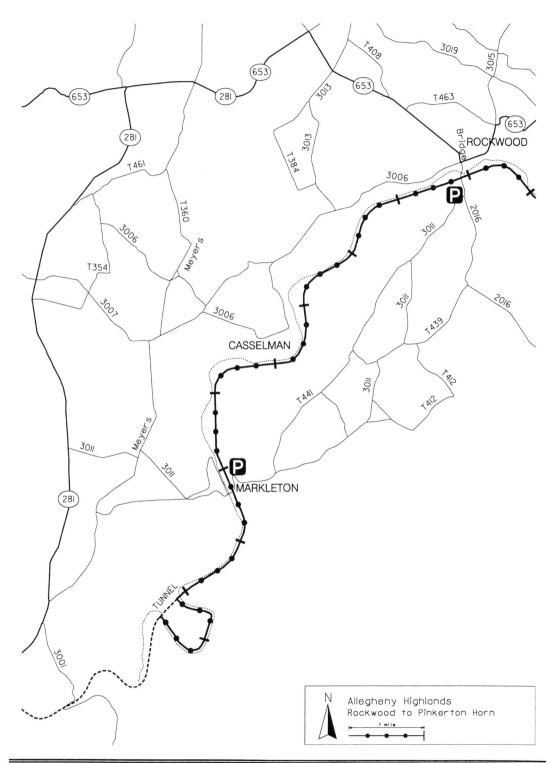

Allegheny Highlands
Rockwood to Pinkerton Horn

1 mile

Swimming, fishing: Unsupervised swimming in the Casselman River. Unfortunately, a mine acid accident has degraded the water quality. This problem is being actively worked on. Many sections of the river have whitewater rapids, so be careful, especially when the water is high.

Winter sports: No snowmobiles. Cross-country skiing is good, as the trail is sheltered and holds snow. The parking lot at Rockwood is plowed regularly.

Maps, guides, other references

Trail Book '95: A Users Guide to the Youghiogheny River Trail and the Allegheny Highlands Trail. Available from the trail councils and many local businesses.

USGS Topographic Maps: Meyersdale, Burdock, Rockwood, Markleton. When the un-developed sections are finished, you'll also need Frostburg, Wittenberg, and Confluence.

Trail organization

Trail Manager for Allegheny Highlands Trail (Casselman River Section)

Hank Parke
Somerset County Rails to Trails Association
829 North Center Av
Somerset PA 15501-1029

(814) 445-6431
(814) 443-4313 (fax)

Membership: $20/year individual or family

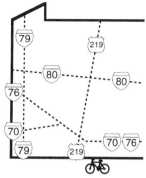

Chesapeake and Ohio Canal Towpath

Cumberland Maryland to Washington DC

The Chesapeake and Ohio Canal Towpath was built between 1828 and 1850, opening progressively from Washington toward Cumberland as sections were completed. This was also the heyday of railroad development, and the C&O Canal competed with the B&O Railroad for both business and right of way. 74 manually-operated lift locks raised the canal from nearly sea level to an elevation of 605 feet at Cumberland.

Floods in January and September of 1996 caused over $20 million in damage to the towpath. The entire towpath is open again, except for a detour near Dam 4 (mile 85) that remains from 1972 flooding. Much of the 184.5-mile length is now in reasonable condition, but some sections still require a mountain bike.

The canal was always vulnerable to flood damage. The devastation from the great flood in 1924, together with competition from railroads, spelled its doom. It is now a National Historical Park. The towpath has been restored, and in some areas the canal has been re-watered. Many traces of the canal era remain, most notably locks, lockmaster's houses, aqueducts, dams, and weirs that controlled water levels. Indeed, the particular attraction of this trail is the extensive evidence of a bygone transportation era.

Chesapeake and Ohio Canal Towpath	
Location	Washington DC to Cumberland Md
Trailheads	Hancock, Paw Paw, Cumberland, many other points closer to Washington
Length, Surface	184.5 miles; mostly packed dirt
Character	Usually uncrowded, rural, mostly shady, flat
Usage restrictions	Horses ok from Swains Lock to Cumberland, but not in campsites or campgrounds; no motorized vehicles; no snowmobiles
Amenities	Rest rooms, water, bike rental, food, camping, swimming, fishing
Driving time from Pittsburgh (to Cumberland)	2 hours 15 minutes southeast

As a trail, it's much like a two-track dirt road, progressively smoother the closer you get to Washington. Avoid riding within two days of heavy rain. Road crossings are relatively far apart, and the busier roads mostly cross over the towpath. Primitive campsites alongside the trail every 5-10 miles offer a pump, picnic table, river access, and portable toilet. The canal alongside has sometimes been restored to hold water, and the path is usually shaded by trees that have grown back since the Canal ceased operations. Wildflowers and birds are abundant. You're likely to see small furry rodents and turtles. Where the canal holds water, you'll also find abundant mosquitoes.

Cumberland is surprisingly convenient to Western Pennsylvania. The western end of the towpath offers one of the best weekend bike camping opportunities in the region.

The trail surface does not encourage speed, but the frequent remnants of the canal operation call for stops to examine the stabilized and restored ruins. Hahn's excellent guidebook is a good companion, especially for historical details.

Local history, attractions

This trail is perhaps the archetype for recreational trail conversions. It was conceived in 1954, when Supreme Court Justice William O. Douglas led 29 people on a hike from Cumberland to Washington along the route of the canal. At the time, the route was being considered for a scenic automobile parkway. Justice Douglas' hike called attention of Washington policy makers to the value of maintaining the route as a sanctuary—and to the need to halt the deterioration of the canal. It was named a National Monument in 1961 and became a National Historical Park in 1971.

The trail is as history-laden as any we've ridden. The remains of the canal have been carefully stabilized or restored. Hahn's guide identifies even the most obscure of features, down to the hundredth of a mile (though his mile marks don't exactly match the Park Service mileposts).

Extensions of the ride

The Georgetown terminus connects to the Washington DC trail network and offers easy access to the Washington & Old Dominion and Mount Vernon trails. You can ride west on the Washington & Old Dominion some 30-odd miles to Leesburg and, at the expense of two miles downhill in fast traffic on busy US15, connect back to the C&O Canal at Whites Ferry. (Some of the W&OD supporters are trying to develop a bike trail along this section of US15).

By the turn of the century, the Allegheny Highlands trail should reach Cumberland to permit a traffic-free trip from Pittsburgh to Washington.

Access points

Vicinity: The C&O Canal follows the Potomac River from Washington to Cumberland. For access from interstate highways, use I270 from Washington to Frederick, I70 from Frederick to Hancock and I68 from Hancock to Cumberland. To reach I68 at Cumberland from Pittsburgh take the PA Turnpike east to Somerset, US219 south to I68, and I68 east to Cumberland. *Alternate route:* From Berlin on US219, it's slightly shorter to take PA160/MD36 directly to Cumberland. *Another alternate route:* Take I79 south to US40, US40 east to I68, and I68 east to Cumberland.

Williamsport trailhead: Leave I70 to go south on I81 near Hagerstown. Exit I81 on US11 in Williamsport. This is East Potomac St. Follow it 1.1 miles west to center of town, turn left for 1 block on West Salisbury St, turn right for 3 blocks into River Front Park.

Hancock trailhead: Take the Hancock exit from I68. Start east on E Main St. For the first few blocks a paved parallel back street follows the towpath on the opposite side of the canal. Follow signs to the picnic area.

Cumberland trailhead: Take the main Cumberland exit from I68 and follow signs to the Western Maryland Train Station. Park in the lot. The trail leaves from the platform one story up. If you're using the alternate route and entering Cumberland on MD36, continue straight to the train station; don't follow AltUS40 over the overpass.

Other trailheads: For access closer to Washington, consult the park brochure.

Amenities

Rest rooms, water: Rest rooms and water at information centers. Water pump and portable toilets at hiker/biker campgrounds every 5-10 miles and also at major access points. The water is drawn from wells and treated by the park service. Sometimes it tastes strongly of iodine; we've seen oatmeal, potatoes, and other starchy foods turn blue -- anyone for patriotic spaghetti?

Bike shop, rental: In Cumberland, Hancock, Williamsport, Shepherdstown, Sandy Hook, Leesburg, Swains Lock, Cabin John, and the Georgetown section of Washington.

Restaurant, groceries: Within a few blocks of the trail at Cumberland, Paw Paw (W Va side of river), Little Orleans, Hancock, Williamsport, Shepherdstown (W Va side of river), Sandy Hook, Harpers Ferry (W Va side of river), Brunswick, Point of Rocks, Whites Ferry, Seneca, and many places as you enter Washington.

Camping, simple lodging: Hiker/biker campgrounds (no road access) every 5-10 miles for tourers. Primitive automobile camping along the canal at Spring Gap, Fifteen Mile Creek (Little Orleans), McCoys Ferry, and Antietam Creek. Camping near the canal also available at Fort Frederick and Brunswick. Lodging in Cumberland, Hancock, Williamsport, Shepherdstown.

Swimming, fishing: The canal water isn't attractive. Many swimming and fishing spots along the Potomac river, especially near campgrounds. Be careful if the water is high.

Winter sports: Cross-country skiing; best chance of snow is at the western end, in the mountains. No snowmobiles.

Trail organization

Superintendent
C&O Canal National Historical Park
Box 4
Sharpsburg MD 21782
(301) 739-4200

For free list of publications or to order:
Parks and History Association
PO Box 40929
Washington DC 20016
(202) 472-3083

Maps, guides, and other references

Trail brochure, *Chesapeake and Ohio Canal Official Map and Guide*

Thomas F. Hahn. *Towpath Guide to the C&O Canal.* American Canal and Transportation Center 1991, 226 pages. (Available at Park Service information centers in Georgetown, Great Falls Tavern, Hancock, and Cumberland.)

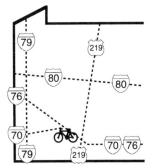

Indian Creek Valley Hiking and Biking Trail

Along Indian Creek in Fayette County

The trail runs along the east bank of Indian Creek, nestled in the valley between Chestnut Ridge and Laurel Ridge. A 5-mile segment from Champion to Indian Head is currently finished. The developed portion of the trail has a variety of surfaces, from crushed limestone to cinders. It has more grades and curves than you'd expect from a rail-trail.

The route was developed between 1906 and 1910 as the Indian Creek Valley Railroad, which carried passengers and freight down Indian Creek to meet the B&O Railroad on the north side of the Youghiogheny River. Above Melcroft, the primary freight came from the logging industry; below Melcroft it came from the mining industry. Since the freight was mostly headed downhill, this railroad could tolerate relatively steeper grades than most.

From Champion the trail runs south for about a mile through woods, then comes into sight of Mountain Pines Resort, an immense campground. Adjacent to the swimming pool at the back of the campground, a footbridge connects the campground and the trail. The trail then passes some homes and camps near Nebo, where it's called C-H Blvd.

Half a mile later, the trail passes a lake, then crosses Fowl Hill Rd (which leads to Melcroft) and enters the woods. At present, you can ride out the road and a short distance on PA381/711 for amenities. Salt Lick Township is trying to finish a railroad spur, including a trestle across Indian Creek, to provide an off-road connection to a park at Melcroft.

Another pastoral mile and a half brings you to some picnic tables overlooking the creek. Shortly thereafter, the trail emerges from the woods at the auto junk yard just north of Sagamore. Another mile brings you to the Indian Head trailhead on Hull St.

Indian Creek Valley Hiking and Biking Trail	
Location	Champion to Indian Head, Saltlick Township, Fayette County
Trailheads	Champion, Indian Head
Length, Surface	5 miles developed, 6 planned; crushed limestone
Character	Little-used, wooded, shady, flat to rolling
Usage restrictions	No motorized vehicles; no horses
Amenities	Rest rooms, food, swimming, fishing
Driving time from Pittsburgh	1 hour 15 minutes south-east

To continue on the undeveloped portion of the trail, follow Hull St 300 ft to SR3089. Turn right on SR3089, go one block, and turn left on a dirt road between Resh's store and Indian Ck. This road swings lift, climbs slightly, and crosses the railroad bed. Turn

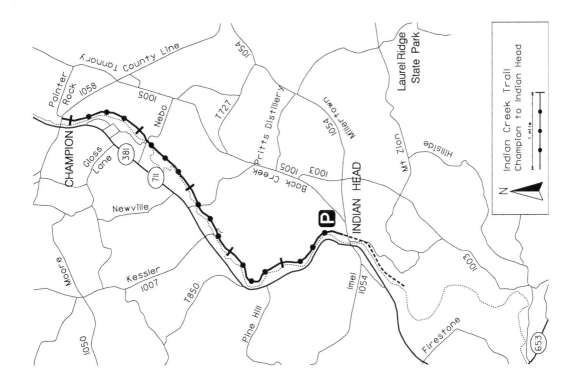

right here, at the sign for ICV Trail. The trail continues for about a mile to the Salt Lick Township line. Salt Lick Township will extend the finished trail to the township line in spring 1996. Springfield Township does not currently plan to develop the portion of trail that runs from the township line to the Youghiogheny River.

Access points

Vicinity: Directions begin headed south on PA711/PA381 from the point where they come together near Jones Mills. To reach this point from Pittsburgh, take the PA Turnpike to Donegal and go east on PA711, then turn south on PA711/PA381.

Champion trailhead: From the junction of PA711 with PA381, follow PA711/PA381 south for about 1.3 miles to Champion. Turn left (east) on SR1058. The trailhead is across from the US Post Office about a quarter mile down SR1058.

Indian Head trailhead: From the junction of PA711 with PA381, follow PA711/PA381 south for about 6 miles to Indian Head. Turn left (east) on SR1054. Just past Resh's store, turn left on Hull St, and follow this road past the trailhead to parking near the ballfield. The trailhead is on the opposite side of the ballfield from the river, along Hull St.

Amenities

Rest rooms, water: Rest rooms at C-W Park, the Indian Head access area.

Bike shop, rentals: None

Restaurant, groceries: A chain convenience store with restaurant is about a quarter-mile west of the trailhead at Champion, at the intersection of SR1058 with PA711/PA381. If you take Fowl Hill Rd from the trail to Melcroft, you can turn left on PA711/PA381 to a O&D Market and a gas station or right to the Valley Inn restaurant (this requires only 1/8 mile on the highway). You can get groceries and deli sandwiches at Resh's store across from the park in Indian Head.

Swimming, fishing: Swim at Mountain Pines Resort pool, just across the trail bridge (fee). There's unlikely to be enough water to swim in the creek at any time you'd be there. Good fishing in creek.

Winter sports: Cross-country skiing.

Trail organization

Evelyn Dix, Secretary
Salt Lick Township, PO Box 403
Melcroft PA 15462-0403

(412) 455-2866

Maps, guides, other references

USGS Topographic Maps: Seven Springs, Donegal.

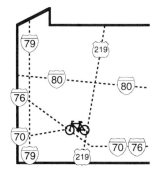

PW&S Railroad Bike Trail

Forbes State Forest and adjacent state parks in Westmoreland and Somerset Counties

Forbes State Forest and the adjacent State Parks (Linn Run, Laurel Mountain, and Laurel Ridge) maintain a network of snowmobile trails and forest service roads though the second-growth forest along Laurel Hill. Much of this network serves as a mountain biking system the rest of the year. Bicycling is allowed *only* on the designated trails (plus, of course, on roads open to automobiles). Bikes are specifically prohibited on the yellow-blazed Laurel Highlands Hiking Trail, which intersects the PW&S system at several places. Currently, the official mountain biking map shows about 15.4 miles of road (mostly dirt) and 19 miles of motor-free trail open north of the PA Turnpike (I76) and south of US30. These trails are marked to indicate their difficulty as "novice" (green ●), "advanced" (blue ■), or "expert" (black ▲). Most of the motor-free trails are rough, rocky, and steep -- true mountain biking trails. Most of the wide easy trails are on lightly-traveled roads. This trail system, then, is unlike virtually all the other trails in this guide.

Within the PW&S network, 6.5 miles follow the route of the former Pittsburgh, Westmoreland, and Somerset Railroad. This includes 3.9 miles along Linn Run Rd, 1.8 miles along Laurel Summit Rd, and 0.8 mile closed to motor vehicles (the "Old PW&S Grade"). Linn Run Rd follows the PW&S railroad for most of the way from Linn Run State Park to the top of the hill. One place where the road deviates from the railroad is near the ranger's residence; two others are at the safety switches at the steep part of the hill. The PW&S grade along Linn Run Rd is quite steep by railway standards—up to 12%.

The low point on the trail system is at the eastern edge of Linn Run State Park on Linn Run Rd. Here a quarry supplied "bluestone" to make the cobblestones that paved many Pittsburgh streets. Quarry Trail emerges here after its final steep descent.

Traces of two original safety switches from the PW&S can be found about a mile southeast (uphill) from the park boundary, where Linn Run Rd crosses Linn Run (from south to north if you're going uphill). At a parking lot here, Fish Run Trail (no bikes) runs well above the road, emerging half a mile later at the lower of the two safety switches. Here Fish Run Trail crosses over to the south side of the road for half a mile and becomes a bike trail. This is the Fish Run-Water Station area; it is on the steepest part of the hill and is one of the finest segments of the original grade. The railroad grade crosses the creek four times in this half-mile, twice on original stone culverts and twice on timber replicas of railroad bridges. The remains of another safety switch and associated features can be seen on the upper end of this half-mile segment. The switches were kept in the safety position and changed manually to let trains pass. Since the train had to stop at each safety switch, these were natural places for water stops as well. Traces of the railroad pond are about 100 yards upgrade from the upper timber bridge. An interpretive area will be developed here. Bikes are permitted on Fish Run Trail only on the half-mile section on the south side of the road. When Fish Run Trail returns to Linn Run Rd, it crosses and becomes hikers-only again; bikes remain on the road.

At Laurel Summit, the PW&S forks. The left branch goes north on Laurel Summit Rd. The right branch is gated to exclude motor vehicles; it starts gently downhill on a wide flat trail. Regrettably, there's only 0.8 miles of it. The portions of the railroad grade on roads are surfaced in dirt and gravel; automobile traffic is light and reasonably slow. These portions are not terribly interesting, but the short segments on Fish Run Rd and on the old railroad grade in the woods are quite pleasant.

Of the 26.5 miles of the trail system that are not on the railroad grade, 8.3 are on dirt and gravel roads that carry even less traffic than Linn Run Rd and Laurel Summit Rd. The surfaces tend to be rough, and there are several significant hills. The elevation change on Linn Run Rd from the low point on the west to the ridge is over 1000'; on the east side it's over 600'.

This leaves a little over 18 miles of serious mountain biking. It's one of the best mountain biking systems in the region, mostly marked and signed "advanced" (blue ■), or "expert" (black ▲). Take a mountain bike and be prepared to take care of yourself and your bike in rugged and remote terrain.

The Laurel Summit Picnic area makes a good base of operations for excursions on the interconnected loops. It is, of course, near the top of the loops.

PW&S Railroad Hiking-Biking Trail	
Location	Forbes State Forest and adjacent state parks, Cook and Ligonier Townships, Westmoreland County; Jenner and Lincoln Township, Somerset Counties
Trailheads	Linn Run Rd, Laurel Summit Rd
Length, Surface	6.5 miles of 34.3-mile network on abandoned rail line; dirt
Character	Uncrowded, wooded, sunny, hilly, very rugged
Usage restrictions	Snowmobiles permitted
Amenities	Rest rooms, water, bike rentals
Driving time from Pittsburgh	1 hour 30 minutes

Local history, attractions

This entire area was clear-cut in the first decade of the 20th century to supply hardwood to a sawmill in Ligonier, then largely burned over. The Pittsburgh, Westmoreland, and Somerset RR was established to haul the timber. It operated from 1899 to 1916. Passenger service was added so people could visit the mountain. Later, the railroad carried bluestone from the quarry to Pittsburgh for paving streets. The main line of the railroad ran from Rector to Somerset. It's relatively steeper than most of the area's railroads, and two level "safety switches" were built along Linn Run to stop runaway cars. Remains of these can still be seen along Fish Run trail, parallel to Linn Run Rd; one is on each side of the road (only the part of the trail to the south of the road is open to bicycles). The state acquired 6000 acres of Byers-Allen Lumber Company land in 1912 for $2/acre, rehabilitated the forest, and stocked it with white-tailed deer. This was the first forest preserve in the Ohio River drainage of Pennsylvania.

Development plans

The 1994 master plan calls for a 46-mile network including six interconnected loops between the Laurel Mountain Ski area and the PA Turnpike. Four of these connected loops, totaling about 34 miles, are now available. The additional loops are slated to include one at the ski area (4 miles) and a connector to the South Penn RR in Somerset County (7 miles).

In the winter, the snowmobile trails north of the PA Turnpike connect with the snowmobile trails to the south using the Laurel Highlands Hiking Trail bridge over the Turnpike. The ranger at Linn Run State Park advises us that this bridge is *not* open to bicycles, so this connection is not available to cyclists.

Access points

Vicinity: Directions begin at the intersection of US30 with PA711 headed east on US30 in Ligonier. To reach this point from Pittsburgh, take the PA Turnpike and exit eastbound on US30 at Greensburg.

Linn Run trailhead: From Ligonier, continue east for 2.0 miles on US30. Turn south (right) on PA381 and go 3.0 miles to Linn Run Rd in Rector. Turn east (left) on Linn Run Rd in Rector, go 2.7 miles up Linn Run Rd to enter Linn Run State Park, and park in any lot as you go up the hill. The Quarry Trail parking lot is 4.0 miles past Rector on this road, just east of the state park boundary.

Laurel Mountain trailhead: From Ligonier, continue east for about 8 miles on US30. When US30 crests the ridge, turn south (right) on Summit Rd and go about 2 miles to the large parking area at the entrance to Laurel Mountain State Park or 0.4 miles farther to parking by the Ski Patrol warming hut.

Amenities

Rest rooms, water: In Linn Run State Park and Laurel Summit picnic area.

Bike shop, rental: Rentals at large parking lot on Laurel Summit Rd near entrance to Laurel Mountain Ski Area and in Laughlintown. Bike shops on W Main St in Ligonier and on US30 near Latrobe.

Restaurant, groceries: In Ligonier, Laughlintown, and Rector.

Camping, simple lodging: Linn Run State Park has ten rustic cabins available for weekly and half-weekly rental.

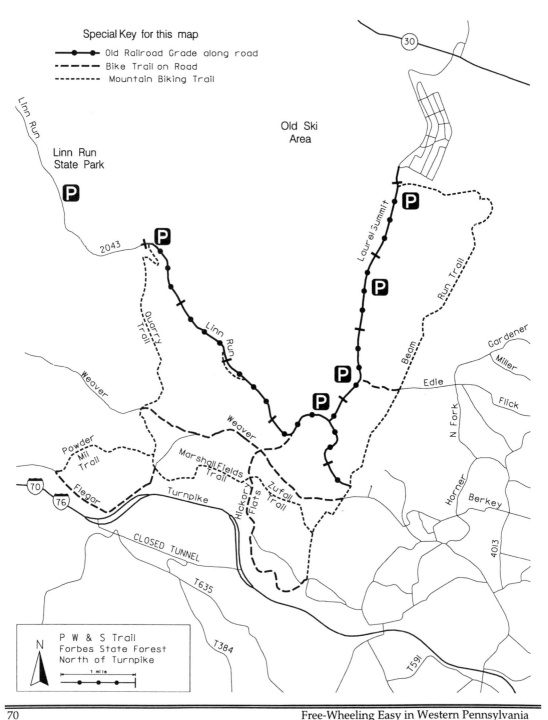

Special Key for this map
━━●━● Old Railroad Grade along road
━ ━ ━ Bike Trail on Road
- - - - Mountain Biking Trail

Old Ski Area

Linn Run

Linn Run State Park

P

30

2043

P

P Laurel Summit

P

Quarry Trail

Linn Run

Beam Run Trail

Gardener

Miller

P

Edie

Flick

Weaver

P

P

Weaver

N Fork

Powder Mil Trail

Marshall Fields Trail

Hickory Flats

Zufall Trail

Horner

Berkey

70

Flegar

Turnpike

76

4013

CLOSED TUNNEL

T635

T384

T591

N

P W & S Trail
Forbes State Forest
North of Turnpike

1 mile

Swimming, fishing: No swimming. Near the lower end of Quarry Trail at Linn Run Rd, there is a set of acid rain treatment wells operated by the Loyalhanna Watershed Association and the State Park. Linn Run is stocked with trout downstream from this treatment facility

Winter sports: Most of these trails are designated snowmobile routes. A separate system of cross-country ski trails (which are not open to bicycles) weaves between the snowmobile routes in the same area.

Trail organization

Trail development

Lysle S. Sherwin, Executive Director
Loyalhanna Watershed Association
114 South Market St
PO Box 561
Ligonier, PA 15658-0561
(412) 238-7560

Operations

District Forester
Forbes State Forest
PO Box 519
Laughlintown PA 15655

(412) 238-9533

Maps, guides, other references

The PW&S Railroad Bike Trail, trail brochure, color-coded to show trail difficulty, from Loyalhanna Watershed Association ($2.00 by mail).

Trail map based on topographic map available from Linn Run State Park office and bicycle rental shops.

Forbes State Forest Public Use Map and Laurel Highlands Snowmobile Trail System Map available from Forbes State Forest.

USGS Topographic Maps: Ligonier, Bakersville.

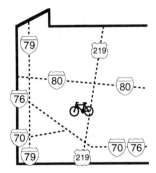

Ghost Town Trail

Along Blacklick Creek from Dilltown to Nanty Glo, with spur from Rexis to White Mill Station in Indiana and Cambria Counties

The Ghost Town Trail runs alongside Blacklick Creek and its South Branch from Dilltown to Nanty Glo, with a spur up North Branch Blacklick Creek from Rexis to White Mill Station. A 10' crushed limestone trail runs through woods, former mining towns, and the remnants of coal mines. Trail landscaping is still in progress, but 10 benches already provide resting places.

The trail is named for five ghost towns, once-thriving mining towns along the railroad that were all abandoned by the 1930s. The Eliza Furnace in Vintondale still remains, as do a few original houses and foundations of mine buildings. The area shows the heritage of the Blacklick Creek valley, which includes railroads, mining, iron making, and lumbering. Much of the trail is in State Game Lands, so wildlife and wildflowers are abundant. Several original railroad mileposts remain; they're about a tenth of a mile east of the trail mileposts.

The main line of the trail follows the route of the 1903 Ebensburg and Blacklick Railroad for 12 miles from Dilltown to Nanty Glo. From Dilltown to Wheatfield the trail runs through scenic woodland, crossing Mardis Run (mile 0 from Dilltown), the new Blacklick Valley Natural Area, Clarke Run (mile 1.7), and Dobson Run (mile 2) before joining Blacklick Creek at Wheatfield (mile 2.4). A historical marker at Wheatfield describes the iron furnace that once operated near here. From Wheatfield through Wehrum to Rexis, the trail lies between a cliff and the river. The location of Wehrum (mile 3.6) can be recognized from the road crossing at SR2013, but there is no trace of the town; the site is private and not open to the public. You can, however, see the remains of a riverside structure, the race for a coal-washing plant, a tenth of a mile to the east. Between Wehrum and Rexis two large mine gob heaps adjoin the trail (miles 4.0-4.1 and 5.0-5.6). They reflect the history of the region but detract somewhat from the scenic value of the trail. Laurel Run (mile 5) crosses just before the second gob pile. The location of the ghost town Lackawanna #3 is also in this area.

The trail forks at Rexis (mile 5.8), with the main trail going right across a bridge to the Eliza Furnace at the edge of Vintondale (mile 6.0); the left fork here is the spur trail up the North Branch. On the main trail, the well-preserved Eliza Furnace (National Register Site, 1846-49) is located on the Cambria/Indiana county line. The furnace was constructed of dry fitted stone, 32 feet high, 32 feet wide, and 31 feet deep. It still boasts its original heat exchange pipes and sits in a well-tended grassy meadow ready for a picnic. A recent grant from the Southwestern Pennsylvania Heritage Preservation Commission will support preservation and historical exhibits here. An archeological site survey identified traces of some of the associated buildings; development of the Eliza Furnace Historic Site will identify and interpret some of these. In the creek just west of the furnace, water bubbles up from the creekbed. This is a set of boreholes drilled to lower the water level in the mine and relieve basement flooding in some homes in Vintondale. The whitish color is an aluminum precipitate.

From Eliza Furnace, the trail follows a grassy embankment beside the road to Vintondale. Where the road crosses the bridge (mile 6.3), the trail swings left along a bench cut into the hillside for 100 ft, then enters a large flat area to pass a loading platform in front of a mine portal (mile 6.6). The trail continues across South Branch Blacklick Creek (mile 7.0) and alongside yet another gob heap (mile 7.1-7.2). The trail then passes a cattail field and cranberry bog (mile 7.3) as it enters State Game Lands #79 and enters the most scenic section. The trail begins to climb noticeably, with a gradient here of 2-3%. You pass the location of the ghost town of Bracken (mile 8.1). This area has reportedly been haunted by the "Lady in White" since she was killed by her lover in the early part of the century.

Ghost Town Trail	
Location	Along Blacklick Creek from Dilltown to Nanty Glo, Buffington Township in Indiana County, Blacklick and Jackson Townships and Vintondale and Nanty Glo Boroughs in Cambria County
Trailheads	Dilltown, Wehrum, Vintondale, Twin Rocks, Nanty Glo
Length, Surface	19.5 planned, 15.5 miles finished, crushed limestone
Character	Uncrowded, wooded, shady, flat (2-3% grade on eastern leg)
Usage restrictions	Horses by permit only; no motorized vehicles; no snowmobiles
Amenities	Rest rooms, water, bike rental, food
Driving time from Pittsburgh	1 hour 20 minutes east

After Bracken, you climb along the creek until it swings away from the trail where a railroad siding once served a strip mine (mile 9.4). Here you go through an impressive cut with a coal seam undercutting the rocks on top (mile 9.5). The trail crosses the creek again on a bridge dated 1916 (mile 9.6) before arriving at the road just south of Twin Rocks (mile 9.7). Here the trail leaves the woods and passes between homes and the river for the last two miles to Nanty Glo. The Welsh spelling is Nant-y-Glo, meaning "streams of coal". On the return trip, you can coast from the 1916 bridge (mile 9.6) almost all the way to the cattail field (mile 7.3).

The spur that takes off at Rexis follows the route of the Cambria and Indiana Railroad for about 4 miles to US422 near White Mill Station. Much of the route runs through State Game Lands #79. A few ruins are visible along the trail. The most notable is a stone building with a railroad platform 2.3 miles from Rexis that was a stone quarry weighing station (privately owned). As of late 1995, the trail surface was complete. However, the bridge near Red Mill Station (2.4 miles from the fork at Rexis), which was destroyed in the 1977 flood, is still out. The bridge is scheduled to be replaced in 1996.

Local history, attractions

The trail corridor is rich in history of the mining, iron, and lumbering industries of the valley. Five ghost towns lie along the trail:

- Armerford and Scott Glen were early mining communities west of Dilltown.
- Wehrum (Lackawanna #4) formerly provided 230 homes, a store, bank, and other services for the Lackawanna Coal and Coke Company. The town was abandoned in the 1930s, and one house remains of the 250 that once stood here. It was located where SR3013 crosses Blacklick Creek; the name still appears on some maps. It's private property now.
- Lackawanna #3 was a short-lived "coal patch" town in the area known as Edward's Flats between Wehrum and Rexis.
- Bracken was a small community between Vintondale and Twin Rocks operated by the Commercial Coal Company.

Eliza Furnace greets you in winter as well as summer

Eliza Furnace operated from 1846 to 1849. At its peak, over 90 people and 45 mules produced about 1080 tons of iron a year. Producing one ton of pig iron required about 2-3 tons of iron ore, 1-1.5 tons of charcoal, and 2.5 tons of limestone. One day's charcoal supply for the furnace required the wood from about one acre of forest. This is one of the best-preserved hot blast furnaces in the state and one of the few anywhere with its hot blast coils (the radiator-shaped metal structure on top) intact. It was never profitable. Its success was doomed by the poor quality of the local iron ore and the cost of transporting the iron overland to the railroad at Nineveh and Johnstown, coupled with external forces such as lowered tariffs on imported iron and discovery of the higher-quality Mesabi range in Minnesota. An interpretive sign near the furnace provides more information. Plans call for an extensive interpretive exhibit surrounding the furnace.

Another iron furnace was located near Wheatfield, but no traces remain. A historical marker at the Wheatfield intersection describes the furnace. A third furnace, Buena Vista Furnace, is located along the active railroad to the west of the end of the trail. The furnaces in the valley were charcoal fired, so charcoal furnaces also dotted the valley.

The railroads that preceded this trail and the coal mines that it served came nearly half a century after Eliza Furnace ceased operation. Vintondale itself was established in 1894 as a coal company town.

Judy and Joseph Kovalchick have contributed land for two rail-trails in western PA, this one and the Roaring Run Trail. They own the Kovalchick Corporations and learned about the rails-to-trails movement in 1989 when Roaring Run Watershed approached them about donating a 4-mile corridor in Apollo. In 1984, they had acquired the route along Blacklick Creek for salvage. In September 1991 they deeded a 15.5-mile corridor, formerly the Ebensburg & Blacklick Railroad, along Blacklick Creek to Indiana County and the Northern Cambria Community Development Corporation (NORCAM). The trail is being developed by Indiana County Parks and NORCAM with help from local citizens of the Cambria and Indiana Trail Council and grants from America's Industrial Heritage Project and ISTEA. The Cambria and Indiana Railroad donated the Rexis spur, formerly the Blacklick & Yellowcreek RR..

Extensions of the Ride

For variety, SR2012 and SR2013 parallel the trail from Dilltown to Rexis. Sometimes they are on the same side of Blacklick Creek as the trail, sometimes on the other. They are lightly traveled and provide a paved alternative. SR3047 parallels the trail from Vintondale to Twin Rocks. Traffic appears to be light, but it's a little heavier than on SR2012 and SR2013. The parallel road from Twin Rocks to Nanty Glo is the rather busier PA271.

Dirt roads in State Game Lands #79 may provide opportunities for extensions of the trip. Most start with brisk climbs of 3-600 feet, but the road that crosses the trail at Bracken provides a gentler access. If you turn at Bracken to cross the river, you can ride a 5-mile loop up, along the ridge, and back down to Eliza Furnace. This is only suitable for mountain bikers with good technical riding skills plus pathfinding and map reading skills. About half a mile after crossing the river on a forest road, take the first right. This climbs northeast for nearly 2 miles with a few steep pitches. A couple of nonobvious turns connect to the power lines on top of the hill; the route follows their cut for a little over a mile. One of the trails to the left will take you back to Bracken. Another (also not obvious) takes you about 2 miles southwest. Another tricky turn puts you on a steep, very technical half-mile hill down to Eliza furnace. If you try this, take the topo map.

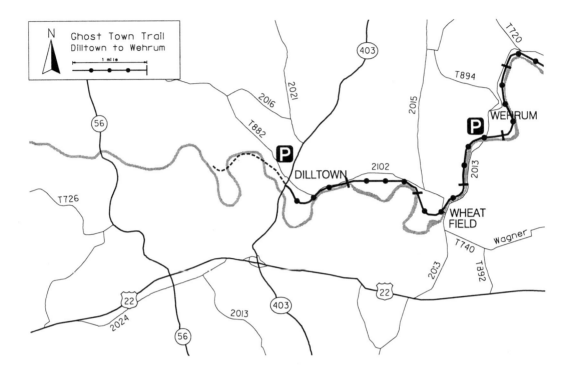

Development plans

Plans call for access areas with parking, water, rest rooms, interpretive exhibits, and benches or picnic tables at Dilltown, Wehrum, Rexis/Vintondale, Twin Rocks, Nanty Glo, and White Mill Station. The missing 105-foot Red Mill Bridge that interrupts the spur trail to White Mill Station on US422 is scheduled to be replaced in 1996. The Eliza Furnace area will be developed as an interpretive site.

David and Penny Russell (of the Dillweed in Dilltown) have donated 675 acres to Indiana County to form the Blacklick Valley Natural Area. Hiking and equestrian trails will be developed in the area, with access from the trail about a mile east of Dilltown.

The master plan calls for extension of the present trail a mile west from Dilltown (currently impeded by another missing bridge) and three miles east from Nanty Glo.

The Conemaugh Valley Conservancy is working on establishing a greenway from Johnstown to Saltsburg.

Access points

Vicinity: Directions begin eastbound on US22 east of Blairsville, where US119 departs northbound. Note that US22 and US119 are the same road for over 10 miles to the west of this point.

Dilltown (west) trailhead: Go east on US22 from its intersection with US119 for 11.6 miles to PA403. Take the PA403 exit. At the end of the exit ramp turn left (north) and continue 1.4 miles to the trailhead. Parking is on the left (west) side of PA403 shortly after you cross the creek.

Wehrum trailhead: Go east on US22 from its intersection with US119 for 13.8 miles to Moose Hill Rd (SR2013). Turn north (left) on SR2013 and continue 2.6 miles to Wehrum, just after SR2013 crosses the river.

Vintondale and Rexis trailheads: Go east on US22 from its intersection with US119 for 19.0 miles to Chickory Hill Rd (SR3045). Turn north (left) on SR3045 and continue for 3.0 miles to the eastern edge of Vintondale, or 0.9 miles farther to the Rexis parking lot (100 yards west of Eliza furnace, just across the bridge).

Nanty Glo (east) and Twin Rocks trailheads: Go east on US22 from its intersection with US119 for 20 miles to PA271. Turn north (left) on PA271 and continue 1.5 miles to Nanty Glo. Just after crossing South Branch Blacklick Creek, turn left on either side of the Nanty Glo Fire Station and follow the river about one block to the trailhead. Park behind the Municipal Building and Fire Station, at the far end of the lot. To reach Twin Rocks trailhead, follow PA271 2.1 miles through Nanty Glo to SR3047. Turn left on SR3047 to the trailhead parking lot (before crossing the creek).

White Mill Station (end of northeast extension) trailhead: Go east on US22 from its intersection with US119 for 11.6 miles to PA403. Exit northbound on PA403, pass through Dilltown and continue to US422. Turn right on US422 and continue to Vic Miller Rd (White Mill Station). Note that this currently provides access to about a mile and a half of trail; a missing bridge separates you from the rest.

Amenities

Rest rooms, water: Rest rooms and water at Dilltown trailhead. Portable toilets at Rexis, Nanty Glo, and Twin Rocks. Note that the Rexis parking lot is at the intersection of the White Mill spur trail with SR3045, 100 yards west of Eliza furnace.

Bike shop, rentals: Two bike rental shops in Dilltown, Trailside Bicycle shop with rentals on Main St in Vintondale, a rental shop at Rexis, and two rental shops in Nanty Glo. There's also a hardware store in Nanty Glo.

Restaurant, groceries: Snacks in Dilltown at the Dillweed and at bike shops in Vintondale. Convenience store on US22 just east of PA403 (1.5 miles from Dilltown). Grocery store on Main St in Vintondale. Nanty Glo is better developed, with Dolly's Restaurant across from the trailhead and Foodland and Subway stores half a mile or so across the river and south on PA271. The Sheetz store that used to be a block from the trailhead has moved to the intersection of PA271 and US22.

Camping, simple lodging: Dillweed Bed-and-Breakfast in Dilltown. Primitive camping at one location along Rexis spur; check at the Dillweed for details. Private campground near Yellow Creek State Park (10 miles northwest).

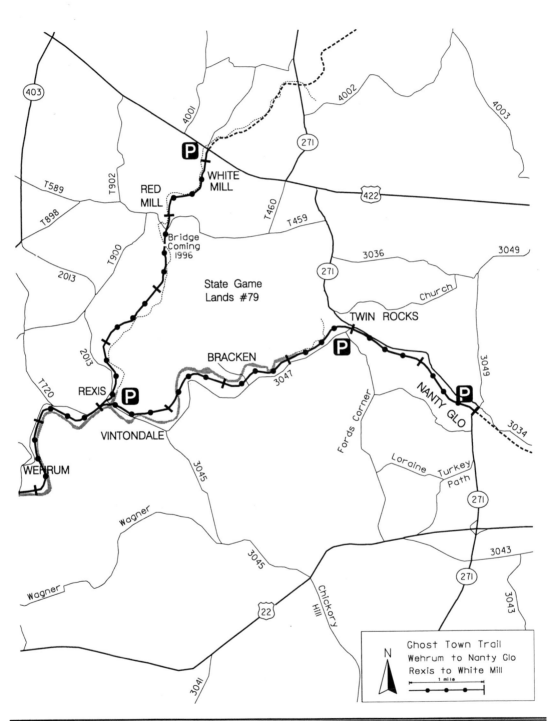

403

4002

4003

4001

271

WHITE MILL

422

T589

T902

RED MILL

T460

T459

T898

T900

Bridge Coming 1996

3036

3049

2013

State Game Lands #79

271

Church

2013

TWIN ROCKS

BRACKEN

3047

3049

T720

REXIS

3049

VINTONDALE

NANTY GLO

WEHRUM

Fords Corner

3034

3045

Loraine Turkey Path

Wagner

271

3045

3043

Wagner

271

22

3043

Chickory Hill

N

Ghost Town Trail
Wehrum to Nanty Glo
Rexis to White Mill

1 mile

3041

Swimming, fishing: Blacklick Creek is the victim of long-standing acid mine pollution and is considered one of the most polluted streams in Pennsylvania. Some of the smaller creeks have clean water, but others carry the acid drainage that winds up in Blacklick Creek. Swimming is not permitted in any of the clean streams. The upper portions of several tributaries (Mardis Run, Clarke Run, and Downey Run) are stocked with trout by the East Wheatfield Cooperative Fish Nursery.

Winter sports: Cross-country skiing on trail and in State Game Lands. Cross-country ski rentals in Dilltown (call Patty White at (814) 446-5928). Snowmobiles not permitted on trail but are permitted in State Game Lands.

Trail organizations

Support Group

C&I Trail Council
PO Box 11
Dilltown PA 15929

Memberships:
$10/year individual; $12/year family

Operations, Indiana County

Ed Patterson
Indiana County Parks
Blue Spruce Park Rd
Indiana PA 15701-9802

(412) 463-8636

Operations, Cambria County

NORCAM (Cambria County)
10th & Philadelphia St
Barnesboro PA 15714

(814) 948-4444

Maps, guides, other references

Trail brochure.

Eliza Iron Furnace interpretive brochure.

Denise Dusza Weber. *Delano's Domain: A History of Warren Delano's Mining Towns of Vintondale, Wehrum and Claghorn.* To buy reprint, write 291 Olive St, Indiana PA 15701.

USGS Topographic Maps: New Florence, Vintondale, Nanty Glo, Strongstown.

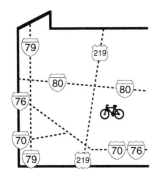

Lower Trail (Juniata River Corridor)

Along the Frankstown Branch of the Juniata River from Alfarata in Huntingdon County to Williamsburg in Blair County

This valley has served as a transportation corridor since it was part of the Frankstown Path, a major Indian route connecting Harrisburg with Kittanning and other towns along the Allegheny River. In subsequent times it has supported a canal, a railroad, and a highway. The route of the former railroad and canal forms the Lower (rhymes with "flower") Trail. This trail runs alongside the Frankstown Branch of the Juniata River without road crossings for 11 miles through forest and farmland. The Juniata River here is more like a creek, often running in shallow riffles near the trail.

Within sight of the Alfarata trailhead, the trail crosses under US22 and heads upstream along the Juniata. Here it squeezes through a small gap in Tussey Mountain. The town here is called Water Street because pack trains used the creek bed through the narrow steep gap.

A mile later, it passes the foundations of structures used to bring stone down from Owens quarry, which you can see high on the hill. Another mile and a half brings you to Goodman quarry, also marked by concrete foundations. Between the two quarries, the canal channel has become the back channel of the creek, usually separated from the main channel by an island. Here, as with most of the remaining traces of the canal, a good imagination will help you visualize the former structures.

About two miles beyond Goodman quarry the trail crosses Fox Run on a handsome stone arch bridge. A view of this bridge from the creek bed is featured in many trail descriptions. Half a mile farther you make the first of two crossings of the Juniata, where the railroad took a shortcut across a peninsula. Just past the second bridge you'll reach the Mt Etna access area, including a bridge over a former mill race. The Mt Etna Iron furnace community is about half a mile from the trail here.

Lower Trail (Juniata River Corridor)	
Location	Alfarata to Williamsburg, Porter and Morris Townships in Huntingdon County; Catherine and Woodbury Townships in Blair County
Trailheads	Alfarata, Etna Iron Furnace, Covedale, Williamsburg
Length, Surface	11 miles, crushed limestone 8' wide with parallel mowed trail
Character	uncrowded, wooded, shady, flat
Usage restrictions	Horses ok; no motorized vehicles
Amenities	Portable toilets, food, swimming
Driving time from Pittsburgh	2 hours 20 minutes east

A mile beyond the access area the trail passes Canal Lock No 61. The walls of the lock are clearly visible. Another mile brings you to numerous foundations that mark the Juniata Limestone Company and its company town, 7 miles from Alfarata and 4 miles from Williamsburg. From here to Williamsburg the traces of the canal are more frequent, including locks and foundations of locktender's houses. Other signs of current use -- farms and houses -- are also more frequent.

The trail is graced by no fewer than four sets of mileage markers -- three from railroads and one for the modern trail. The trail is marked from 0 to 11 in both directions in white numbers on brown posts. The railroad markers are black on white. Two such markers (with different numbering systems) are just north of the Williamsburg parking lot, and others appear along the length of the trail.

Cross-country skier emerging at Alfarata trailhead

Local history, attractions

The Frankstown Path, also called the Allegheny Path or Ohio Path was the major Indian trail across this region. It connected Paxtang (now Harrisburg) with Kittanning and Forks of the Ohio (now Pittsburgh). In this area it followed approximately the same route as US22, and it's known locally as the Kittanning Path. Hunters, trappers, and pioneers later used this route to reach the frontier.

The canal was built in the 1830's as part of the Juniata Division of the Pennsylvania Main Line Canal, which connected Philadelphia to Pittsburgh with three canals, a railroad, and the Allegheny Portage Railway, a combination railroad and inclined plane. The system also included the nearby Allegheny Portage Railroad and further canal works along the Conemaugh and Kiskiminetas Rivers Traces of this part of the canal can also be seen along Roaring Run Trail. Poor management, floods, and the rise of railroads led to the demise of the canal.

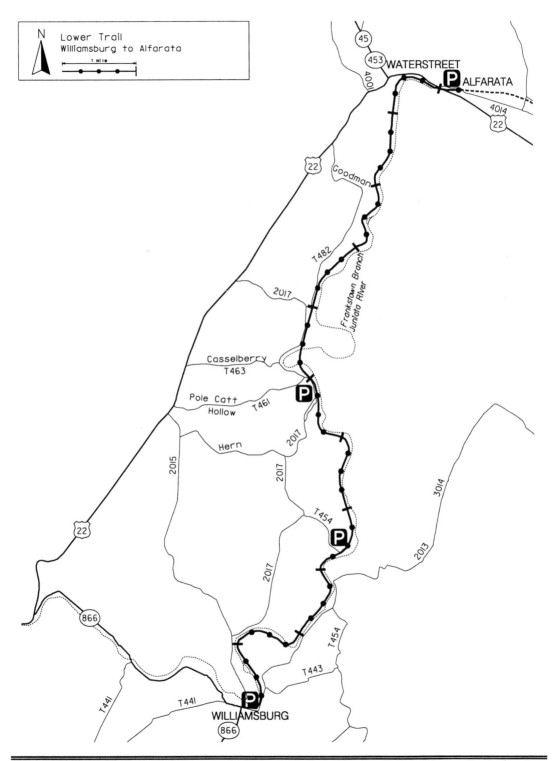

Lower Trail
Williamsburg to Alfarata

1 mile

N

WATERSTREET
ALFARATA
Goodman
Frankstown Branch
Juniata River
Casselberry
T463
Pole Catt
Hollow
Hern
Williamsburg

45
453
400
4014
22
22
T482
2017
T461
2017
2015
2017
2017
3014
2013
T454
T454
T443
T441
T441
866
866

As technology gave railroads superiority over canals, the Pennsylvania Railroad system purchased the entire Mainline Canal system in 1857. In 1879 the Petersburg Branch of the Pennsy was built on this corridor. It operated until 1979 and was abandoned in 1982. In 1990, T. Dean Lower provided funding to purchase the corridor as a rail-trail.

Access points

Vicinity: Directions begin headed east on US22 from its intersection with PA36 in Hollidaysburg. To reach this point from Pittsburgh, go east on US22 past US220, taking care to stay on US22 when it exits at the beginning of the US220 interchange.

Alfarata (north) trailhead: Follow US22 18.6 miles east from PA36. Turn left on SR4014 (to Alfarata) and go 0.4 miles to trailhead parking. The left turn from US22 to SR4014 is 0.7 miles after the intersection of US22 and PA45/453.

Williamsburg (south) trailhead: Follow US22 9.1 miles east from P36. Turn right on PA866 (to Williamsburg). Follow PA866 into town, where it becomes First St. Remain on First St when PA866 turns right and go two blocks farther to trailhead parking at the intersection of First St and Liberty St. Parking is a total of 3.8 miles from US22.

Amenities

Rest rooms, water: Portable toilets at Alfarata and Williamsburg trailheads.

Bike shop, rental: none

Restaurant, groceries: In Williamsburg. Convenience store a block from Williamsburg trailhead.

Camping, simple lodging: Family cabins at Canoe Creek State Park.

Swimming, fishing: Swimming in Frankstown Branch Juniata River. Quality of fishing unknown.

Winter sports: Cross-country skiing

Trail organization

Jennifer Barefoot or Palmer Brown, President
Rails-to-Trails of Blair County
PO Box 592
Hollidaysburg PA 16648-0592
(814) 832-2400
Membership: $10/year individual, $12/year family

Maps, guides, other references

Trail brochure, available at trailheads

USGS Topographic Maps: Spruce Creek, Williamsburg

Trails North: Upper Allegheny Valley

Allegheny Valley Rail Trail System

An extensive network of rail-trails is growing in Venango and Clarion Counties under the leadership of the small but vigorous Allegheny Valley Trails Association. The main stem of this system runs along the Allegheny River as the Allegheny River Trail and the Samuel Justus Trail. The trail council would eventually like to extend the trail southward to connect with the Armstrong Trail below Kennerdell. They also hope for a northward extension along the Allegheny River to Warren and various side lines.

Long-term plans call for the spine along the Allegheny River to be supplemented with the 50-mile Clarion Secondary Trail, running from near Clarion northwest to Sandy Lake near I79. Additional plans include a loop connector from Franklin to Polk, a connector to include the Oil Creek State Park trail, connection to the Old Salem Trail in northern Mercer County, and a 25-mile network in Allegheny National Forest.

The region is protected by both the National Wild and Scenic River program and the Oil Heritage Park program. The Allegheny River from Warren to Oil City and from Franklin to Emlenton is a Wild and Scenic River. The Oil Heritage Park extends along Oil Creek from Titusville to Oil City and along the Allegheny River from Oil City to Emlenton.

If it all works out, this will provide a continuous connection from near Pittsburgh to several points in the northern part of the state. Unfortunately, some parcels along the trail have passed into private ownership, and re-establishing the trail will take a lot of effort. Prospects are good for extending the trail as far south as I80, not so good south of there.

As of late 1995, the Oil Creek State Park and Samuel Justus trails are complete. The Allegheny River Trail is open for 10 miles to near Brandon, paved from Franklin to Belmar. The Clarion Secondary Trail is under development from near Clarion to Pecan. Other parts of the system are proposed or in planning.

Farther south, the Armstrong Trail is officially open, but there has been little trail development and some nearby landowners are opposing trail development. Much of the route is open on the dirt/gravel/ballast railroad access road, now used to reach the numerous summer homes along the Allegheny River. Some traffic control has been installed.

Other trails in the Allegheny basin follow segments of Cowanshannock Ck near Rural Valley, Kiskiminetas River near Apollo, Little Buffalo Ck near Freeport, Lake Arthur near Portersville, Mahoning River near New Castle, and Lake Erie on Presque Isle.

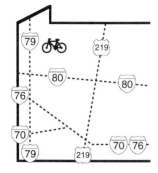

Oil Creek State Park Trail

Petroleum Center to Drake Well Museum near Titusville in Venango County

The birthplace of the oil industry supplies the setting for a ride that combines the natural beauty of Oil Creek Valley's clear trout stream and hemlock-hardwood forest with traces of the oil boom that once dominated the valley. The trail follows the path of the railroad that once carried oil from wells in this and adjacent valleys. But the intervening century has erased most evidence of the industry, and you now rely on interpretive signs along the trail and the Drake Well Museum to pick out the remaining traces.

The trail begins at Petroleum Centre near the SR1004 bridge. It shares a township road with traffic for 0.5 miles, then drops down to Oil Creek and crosses under the Oil Creek and Titusville Railroad. A mile later the trail crosses from the east side of Oil Creek to the west, remaining on the west side for the remainder of the trip. Shortly after crossing the creek, at northbound mile 1.7, is the marker for the historic site of Pioneer. There are also markers for Shaffer Farm (northbound mile 4.4), Miller Farm (northbound mile 5.2), and Boughton (northbound mile 7.5), but few visible traces remain. The most obvious is a rock foundation wall at Boughton. The trail continues northbound to mile 9.7; you can continue on the road to Drake Well Museum.

The trail is asphalt-surfaced, 8.5 feet wide, with a few short hills. It is well populated with interpretive signs, views of Oil Creek, wildlife, picnic tables, benches, and rain shelters. It can be busy to crowded on nice summer weekends.

You're likely to see excursion trains of the Oil Creek and Titusville Railroad across the creek from the trail. If you want to cycle one way and ride the train back, your bike can join you on the train for $1 over your fare ($9 for adults in 1995).

Oil Creek State Park Trail	
Location	South of Titusville, Cornplanter and Cherrytree Townships, Venango County
Trailheads	Petroleum Centre, Drake Well Museum
Surface	9.7 miles; asphalt 8.5 feet wide with parallel ballast treadway
Character	Busy, wooded, shady, very gently rolling
Usage restrictions	No motorized vehicles, no snowmobiles, no horses
Amenities	Rest rooms, water, bike rental, food, fishing
Driving time from Pittsburgh	2 hours 30 minutes north

Development Plans

Plans for the Allegheny Valley Trail system call for incorporating this trail as a segment of its Corry to Franklin leg, but it will take some creativity to get down the Oil Creek valley along PA8.

Watching herons from a bench by the Oil Creek Trail

Local history, attractions

This area is the birthplace of the American oil industry. For centuries, oil occurred naturally on the surface along Oil Creek. In 1859, Colonel Edwin Drake came to the area searching for a quantity source and became the first to drill for oil. On Sunday August 28, his well just south of Titusville struck oil at a depth of 69 feet. Drake Well Memorial Park is on the site of his well.

The next dozen years saw a boom and bust in the local oil industry, with development and demise of entire towns. Petroleum Centre grew suddenly to a population of 3,000 in 1863; the town of Pithole, a few miles to the east, was built between May and September of 1865 and was already vanishing by January of 1866. Both towns are now historical sites where you can visit some of the remaining traces. There were also oil fields at Tarr Farm, Pioneer and Miller Farm, along the bike trail. The Oil Creek Railroad was created to ship oil out of the valley. Miller Farm was terminus of railroad; the world's first successful oil pipeline connected it to Pithole, 5.5 miles to the east.

Oil Creek State Park provides interpretive information, including signs at many points along the trails. Additional attractions include the Drake Well Museum 0.4 miles from the northern end of the trail (admission fee), the Pithole historical site, and the Oil City & Titusville excursion train, which runs on the opposite side of Oil Creek from the trail.

The valley continues to be an oil center: the oldest producing oil well in the country is the McClintock No. 1, owned by Quaker State and located just north of Oil City. It has been producing continuously since August 1861.

Extensions of the ride

Signs at Petroleum Center indicate an antique car museum 2.5 miles east on the township road: start up the trail from Petroleum Center, and when the bike trail leaves the road, stay on the road for 2 more miles. The ghost town of Pithole (with museum) is also east of the park; the map suggests that it's accessible on back roads 2-3 miles beyond the car museum. If you find a good route, let us know.

Access points

Vicinity: Directions begin northbound on PA8 at the end of the bypass around Oil City. To reach this point from Pittsburgh, go north on I79, east on I80, and north on PA8, taking the PA8 bypass around Oil City.

South trailhead (Petroleum Centre): From the northern end of the PA8 bypass, continue north 3.5 miles on PA8 to the turnoff marked for Petroleum Centre at Oil Creek State Park. (The correct turnoff is just *north* of the PA8 bridge over Cherrytree Creek; do not confuse this with the turnoff for Rynd Farm and OC&T RR, which is just *south* of this short bridge.) Turn right toward Petroleum Centre on SR1007. Follow signs for 3.1 miles to a "T" where SR1007 turns left and SR1004 goes right. Turn right on SR1004 and cross Oil Creek. Trailhead parking is just ahead on the left. *Alternate route:* If you are coming southbound from Titusville on PA8, it's faster to reach Petroleum Centre by turning left at the well-marked intersection in Cherrytree, 5.4 miles after you cross Oil Creek just south of Titusville.

North trailhead (Drake Well Museum): From the northern end of the PA8 bypass around Oil City, continue north on PA8 for 14 miles to the stop light at Bloss St, marked for Drake Well Museum. Turn right and continue for just under a mile to trailhead parking on the right (just before Jersey Bridge over Oil Creek).

Other access: If you're truly determined to gain intermediate access, get the park brochure and follow back roads to the Pioneer or Miller Farm historic sites.

Amenities

Rest rooms, water: Rest rooms and water at park office in Petroleum Centre. Latrine along trail just south of the intersection with Miller Farm Rd (northbound mile 4.9). Rest rooms and water at Drake Well Museum.

Bike shop, rentals: No bike shop; rentals Memorial Day to Labor Day, plus weekends in spring and fall at the old Egbert Oil Office at Petroleum Center (south trailhead).

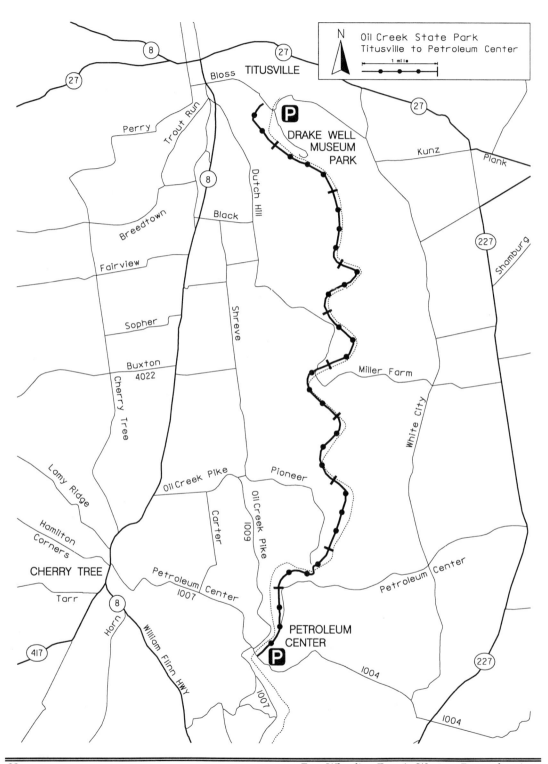

Oil Creek State Park
Titusville to Petroleum Center

1 mile

Restaurant, groceries: Light snacks and soft drinks at rental shop. Soft drink machines at Drake Well Park. Groceries in Rouseville and Titusville.

Camping, simple lodging: Oil Creek Camp Resort: from west side of Oil Creek at Petroleum Centre, up Oil Creek Pike Rd (SR1009) for just over a mile, then follow signs to jog right on Pioneer Rd for 0.1 mile then left for 0.5 miles on Shreve Rd to the campground.

Swimming, fishing: No authorized swimming area in the state park. Oil Creek is one of the largest trout streams in Pennsylvania. It offers prime trout fishing throughout the season and is stocked by the state. Deep pools alternate with productive riffles.

Winter sports: Cross-country skiing on trail and on nearby (hilly) cross-country system. No snowmobiles.

Trail organization

Douglas Finger, Park Manager
Oil Creek State Park
RR 1, Box 207
Oil City PA 16301
(814) 676-5915

Maps, guides, other references

The map in the park's information brochure shows the bike route.

Trail brochure, "Bicycle Trails of Venango County"

USGS Topographic Maps: Titusville South.

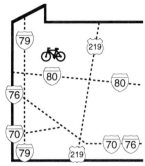

Samuel Justus Recreational Trail

Franklin to Oil City in Venango County

A 9-foot strip of excellent asphalt runs along the former Allegheny Valley Railroad right-of-way between the south bank of the Allegheny River and a wooded bluff. The trail is almost completely flat and runs about 30 feet above the river, affording good views of whatever is happening on the river. Birds and wildflowers are abundant

The trail passes several oil wells, some still operating, and oil storage tanks. Picnic areas between the trail and the river offer shade and picnic tables; they are located 0.7 mile upstream from the Franklin gate and 0.5 mile downstream from the Oil City gate.

The most prominent feature of this trail is River Ridge Farm, located two miles upstream from Franklin. This impressive mansion was built in 1913 by Joseph C. Sibley, who developed the first formula for refining crude oil and later served five terms in the US House of Representatives. The estate originally included 21 other buildings, including a stone campanile near the river. This bell tower still stands, but the eleven bells have been removed. The entrance gate, with "River Ridge Farm" carved across the top, still stands near where a railroad siding served the estate's junction. The estate is now owned by Life Ministries, Inc. It is not closed to the public, but if you choose to visit the grounds, please remember it is private property.

At the Oil City trailhead, the parking area adjoins the sewer plant. Be prepared to hold your nose until you're out of range.

Samuel Justus Recreational Trail	
Location	South side of Allegheny River near Franklin, Cranberry Township, Venango County
Trailheads	Franklin, Oil City
Surface	Reported 5.8 miles, asphalt 8 feet wide with parallel ballast treadway (measured 5.4 miles gate to gate; 9 ft wide)
Character	Uncrowded, rural, mostly sunny, flat
Usage restrictions	Horses ok; no motorized vehicles
Amenities	Portable toilets, bike rental, food, swimming, fishing
Driving time from Pittsburgh	1 hour 45 minutes north

Development plans

Oil City plans to extend the trail from its current end into Oil City, probably in 1997. From the current end at the sewer plant, it will follow the railbed to the marina, then follow the river in a bicycle lane, cross the Allegheny River on a road bridge and Oil Creek on a former railroad trestle, and parallel Oil Creek to a park near the Holiday Inn.

Plans call for eventual extension above Oil City. The proposed route will follow the south side of the Allegheny R northeast from Silverly, cross a bridge just east of the mouth of Oil Ck, and follow the northwest side of the Allegheny R past Trunkeyville, then onward to Warren.

Plans for the Allegheny Valley Trail system also call for connecting to Oil Creek Trail as a segment of the Corry to Franklin leg, but there's no really good corridor down the Oil Creek valley along PA8.

Local history, attractions

The Allegheny Valley Railroad was established to serve the oil industry. Around the turn of the century, it was incorporated in the Pennsylvania Railroad system, and it later became part of Conrail.

The "salt box" house in the parking lot at the Franklin trailhead was moved there when it was rescued from a construction project at its former location on Liberty St in Franklin. This house dates to 1844 and is the only true salt box in the area. This architectural style is characteristic of certain parts of New England and is defined by the roof line, which extends farther down in back than in front. When restored, the house will serve as a visitor and information center for the trail. The Franklin trailhead also offers a "fitness cluster"

Extensions of the ride

The Samuel Justus Trail is part of the emerging Allegheny Valley Trail system. At present, you can continue south on the Allegheny River Trail 5 miles to Belmar (see description).

There should be an interesting architectural tour on the back streets of Franklin. The Debence Antique Music museum has moved to Franklin, at 1261 Liberty St. Check also on the Oil City streets that parallel 1st St (which is too busy to recommend). We have not ridden either of these.

A loop on the south side of the river is unlikely, as the roads up from the trailheads are narrow and somewhat busy.

Access points

Vicinity: Directions begin headed north on US62/PA8 in Franklin. To reach this point from Pittsburgh, go north on I79, east on I80, and north on PA8 to Franklin.

South trailhead (Franklin): In Franklin, when US62/PA8 turns left, stay on US322. Continue 0.3 miles to the next stop light, following US322 left onto 8th St and another 0.3 miles across the Allegheny River. As you leave the bridge, trailhead parking is on your right. Access to the parking lot is a right turn about 0.1 mile past the end of the bridge; it's well marked by a sign for "Samuel Justus Recreational Trail". For bike rental, walk back under the US322 bridge. This is also the (only) trailhead for the Allegheny River Trail.

North trailhead (Oil City): In Franklin, continue on US62/PA8 about 8 miles to the outskirts of Oil City. Follow US62 North when it turns right to cross Allegheny River. After crossing the river, turn right at the second light on West 1st St (SR3025). Go 1.6 miles to the trail turnoff, which is marked "Samuel Justus Recreational Trail" and "Waste Water Treatment Plant" (this is just past the Penelec plant and across from the entrance to Venango Campus of Clarion College). Turn right and follow the road along the sewage plant to park near the trailhead.

Amenities

Rest rooms, water: No water; portable toilets at Franklin trailhead. Rest rooms in Oil City at the PA Fish Commission access: enter Oil City by turning left on Wyllis St, go 2 short blocks downhill to Pa Fish Comm access on Front St (this is the better part of 2 miles from the trail).

Bike shop, rentals: Country Pedalers bike shop with rentals at Franklin trailhead. Rentals at Oil City trailhead.

Restaurant, groceries: Minimal snacks at the bike rental shops. Restaurants and groceries in Oil City and Franklin.

Camping, simple lodging: Motels and B&Bs in Oil City and Franklin.

Swimming, fishing: In Allegheny River. Be careful of current if it's high. Good fishing for bass and walleye.

Winter sports: Cross-country skiing.

Trail organization

Richard A. Castonguay, Secretary
Cranberry Township
PO Box 378
Seneca PA 16346-0378
(814) 676-8812

Maps, guides, other references

Trail brochure, "Bicycle Trails of Venango County"

USGS Topographic Maps: Franklin, Oil City.

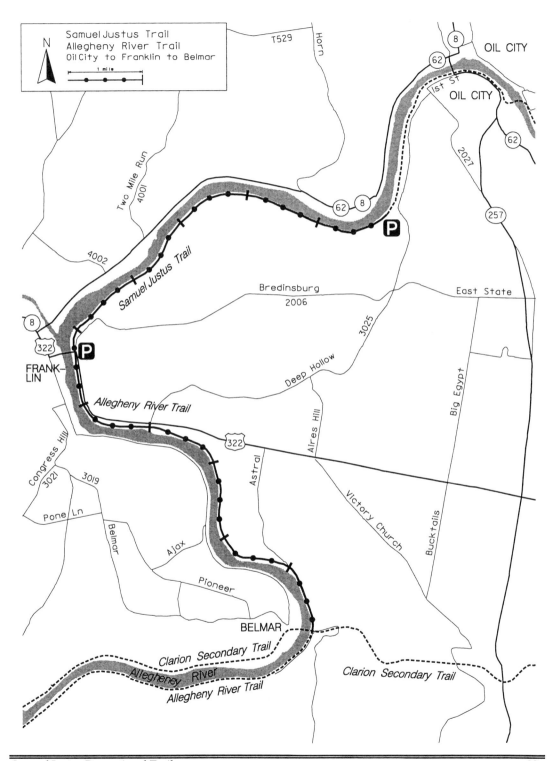

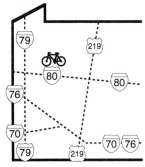

Allegheny River Trail

Franklin to Kennerdell in Venango County

The Allegheny River Trail follows the Allegheny River south from Franklin to Kennerdell. The 5 miles from Franklin to Belmar have an 8'-wide asphalt surface. The 5 miles from Belmar to near Brandon are currently original fill and ballast. They will be finished in crushed limestone or rough asphalt. Plans call for extending the trail toward Kennerdell, at least to the quarter-mile gap a mile north of Kennerdell where land has reverted to adjacent property owners; there is no public access either here or at Kennerdell. We have only ridden Franklin to 2.5 miles past Belmar.

This trail takes you to some of the region's most outstanding rivers. The Allegheny River in this area was added to the National Wild and Scenic Rivers system in 1992. East Sandy Creek, which you cross at Belmar, is on the Pennsylvania Scenic Rivers inventory.

As you leave the parking lot, the trail gradually bears away from US322, finally breaking away at mile 0.6 near the ruins of the former industrial plant. This building, the Whann Litha Springs building, came down in 1995. From here on you have frequent views of the river. In mid-summer 1996, the flat area at mile 1.8 will be a campsite with Adirondack shelters, fire rings, slabs for tents, picnic tables, and canoe access. At mile 2.1 an overlook provides views up and down the Allegheny River with good birdwatching opportunities. Near milepost 2.5 you can see oil pumps and a storage tank beside the trail. At mile 3.8, a rest area with picnic table and fire ring lies below the trail by the river amid remnants of some sort of pipeline operation. The finished trail surface ends at the bridge over East Sandy Creek, 5.1 miles south of Franklin. Just beyond, the trail passes under the Belmar Bridge. Built in 1907, this bridge carried the Clarion Secondary line over the Allegheny River. This line is also being developed as a rail-trail, and a connection between the two at this point is planned for 1996.

Beyond here, the unfinished trail continues toward Brandon on a rough surface of original ballast. The next 5 miles -- almost, but not quite all the way to Brandon -- are scheduled to get a rough paved surface in 1996.

Allegheny River Trail	
Location	Franklin to Kennerdell, Cranberry and Rockland Townships, Venango County
Trailheads	Franklin
Length, Surface	10 miles: 5.1 miles asphalt, 8' wide to Belmar; 4.9 miles original fill and ballast to near Brandon
Character	Uncrowded, rural, mostly sunny, flat
Usage restrictions	Horses ok; no motorized vehicles; no snowmobiles
Amenities	Portable toilets, bike rental, food, swimming, fishing
Driving time from Pittsburgh	1 hour 45 minutes north

Local history, attractions

At least half a dozen Indian paths converged at Venango (now Franklin), but none of them appears to have followed the Allegheny River. The river corridor was originally shaped by French and British fortifications. More recently it provided transportation for the oil and timber industries. The area is included in both the Wild and Scenic Rivers program and the Oil Heritage Park program.

John Wilkes Booth was part owner of an oil well near the trail a mile south of Franklin.

It is reported that Indian God Rock, a large rock at river's edge 4 miles south of Belmar, holds 50 Indian rock carvings dating to AD 1200-1750; this is listed on the National Register of Historic Places. Kennerdell tunnel, just past the southern end of the trail, runs 0.75 miles through the hill; its curve guarantees complete darkness.

Belmar Bridge will carry the Clarion Secondary Trail across the Allegheny River

Extensions of the ride

At Franklin, you can continue north to the edge of Oil City on the Samuel Justus Trail.

An additional 9 miles toward Brandon and eventually the Kennerdell Tunnel is under development but not yet finished as of spring 1996. The first 5 miles of this extension, from Belmar toward but not all the way to Brandon, should be finished in early 1996.

Development plans

The 5-mile segment from the Belmar Bridge (at the mouth of East Sandy Creek) toward, but not quite to, Brandon will be the next section to be developed. Expect 5 more miles of tar-and-chip surface (rough pavement) in the first half of 1996.

The Belmar Bridge across the Allegheny River is also scheduled for development in 1996. The bridge will be repaired and re-surfaced, and a ramp will connect it with the Allegheny River Trail. On the opposite side of the Allegheny River, the bridge will connect with 5 miles of trail that have had the ballast removed, leaving a hard (if rough) surface. This will be the first section of the Clarion Secondary Trail.

Access points

Vicinity: Directions begin headed north on US62/PA8 in Franklin. To reach this point from Pittsburgh, go north on I79, east on I80, and north on PA8 to Franklin.

North trailhead: In Franklin, when US62/PA8 turns left, remain on US322. Continue 0.3 miles to the next stop light, following US322 left onto 8th St and another 0.3 miles across the Allegheny River. As you leave the bridge, trailhead parking is on your right. Access to the parking lot is a right turn about 0.1 mile past the end of the bridge, well-marked by a sign for "Samuel Justus Recreational Trail". For bike rental, walk back under the US322 bridge. This also serves as a trailhead for the Samuel Justus Trail.

Amenities

Rest rooms, water: No water; portable toilets at Franklin trailhead.

Bike shop, rentals: Country Pedalers bike shop with rentals at Franklin trailhead, (814) 432-8055; Ken and Lynn Cochran are active in the Allegheny Valley Trails Association and will provide information on trails or volunteer opportunities.

Restaurant, groceries: Minimal snacks at the bike rental shop. Restaurants and groceries in Franklin.

Camping, simple lodging: Probably in Franklin.

Swimming, fishing: In Allegheny River. Be careful of current if it's high. Good fishing for bass and walleye.

Winter sports: Cross-country skiing.

Trail organization

James Holden or Neal Parker
Allegheny Valley Trails Association
Franklin Area Chamber of Commerce
1256 Liberty St, Suite 2
Franklin PA 16323
Membership: $20/year individual, $25/year family

Maps, guides, other references

Trail brochure, "Bicycle Trails of Venango County"

USGS Topographic Maps: Franklin, Kennerdell

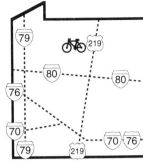

Buzzard Swamp

Southeast of Marienville in Forest County

Allegheny National Forest offers many opportunities for bicycling. They are more rugged than most of the trails in this guide. The Buzzard Swamp area offers a 12-mile network of rolling grassy trails with good opportunities to see wildlife. It provides an easy transition from developed rail-trails to off-road cycling.

In the early 1960's the US Forest Service and the PA Game Commission created a chain of 15 ponds for fish propagation. Now the dikes and meadows around these ponds offer hiking and mountain biking. The trail surface is wide and smooth but unimproved. If you're there soon after a trail is mowed, it's like riding on the lawn. If the grass is high, it's a meadow experience you won't forget. Most of the trails are not blazed, but there are signposts at the intersections. The national forest brochure will help you stay oriented

The area is a special management area that balances wildlife management and recreational opportunities. Fishing in the ponds is encouraged. Entry to the small (40 acre) wildlife propagation is strictly prohibited, but you may peer in from the bordering trails. This is an important link in the Atlantic flyway, so it's a great place to see birds during seasonal migrations. Spring migration brings 20-25 species of waterfowl. You may also see nonmigratory birds, mammals, and reptiles.

Buzzard Swamp itself lies on the southern edge of the area. The higher ground is not swampy, and we found the trails firm. However, mosquitoes thrive here, and they get denser as you approach the swamp. Combined with the lack of tree cover, that makes this a better spring or fall trip than a summer trip.

Buzzard Swamp	
Location	Southeast of Marienville, Jenks Township, Forest County
Trailheads	East and south of Marienville
Length, Surface	12-mile network; mostly mowed grass
Character	Little-used, forest, sunny, rolling
Usage restrictions	No motorized vehicles; no snowmobiles; no horses
Amenities	Fishing
Driving time from Pittsburgh	2 hours 45 minutes northeast

Extensions of the ride

Allegheny National Forest has an extensive network of forest service roads. For the most part, they're dirt or gravel and they carry little traffic. Get the National Forest map from the ranger and pick out your own routes. These roads can be very hilly.

A number of traffic-free trails in Allegheny National Forest are open to bicycles. Several of them incorporate sections of former railroad grades, but many of them are more rugged. They are dispersed through the forest. Get more detailed information from the Forest Service or Rails to Trails.

Access points

Vicinity: Directions begin at the 6-way junction in Marienville, where US62 intersects Loleta Rd and forest service routes FR130 and FR128. To reach this point from Pittsburgh, go north on I79, then east on I80, then northeast on PA66 near Clarion. Marienville is around 20 miles northeast of I80.

North trailhead: At the 6-way junction in Marienville, go east on FR130 for 2.5 miles. Turn right (south) on FR376, a short dirt road that soon terminates in a parking lot.

West trailhead: At the 6-way junction in Marienville, go south on Loleta Rd for 1 mile. Turn left (east) on FR157 and go just over 2 miles to parking at the trailhead.

Amenities

Rest rooms, water: None

Bike shop, rentals: None

Restaurant, groceries: In Marienville

Camping, simple lodging: Allegheny National Forest campgrounds at Loleta, Kelly Pines, Beaver Meadows. Check with the ranger about dispersed camping in Allegheny National Forest. Commercial campground south of Marienville.

Swimming, fishing: No swimming. All the ponds in the area have small and largemouth bass, perch, catfish, crappie, and bluegill.

Winter sports: Cross-country skiing encouraged. Snowmobiles prohibited.

Trail organization

Allegheny National Forest
Marienville Ranger District
HC 2, Box 130
Marienville PA 16239
(814) 927-6628

Maps, guides, other references

Buzzard Swamp Wildlife Viewing & Hiking Area. Trail brochure from Allegheny National Forest.

USGS Topographic Maps: Marienville East

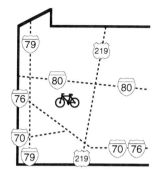

Armstrong Trail

Along Allegheny River from Schenley to Upper Hillville in Armstrong and Clarion Counties

In using this trail, you should be aware that some nearby land-owners question the trail operator's title to the trail and right to use the land. As of January 1996, this disagreement is being litigated. In addition, some sections of the trail may be obstructed or posted. We recommend against trespassing or antagonizing trail neighbors anywhere, but especially so here. Since the status of this matter changes from time to time, you may wish to check with the trail operator about the current status.

Armstrong Trail is planned to run for about 52 miles along the east side of the Allegheny River from Schenley to Upper Hillville, primarily in Armstrong County and partly in Clarion County. Spur trails are planned westward to East Brady and eastward along Red Bank Creek. The trail was acquired and dedicated in 1992. Some improvements have been made, primarily removal of old rails and installation of gates to exclude traffic. It is still an unfinished trail in 1996, suitable only for primitive uses. Many sections are now passable. Where the ballast has been removed the trail surface is rough. Elsewhere it's very rough.

The trail begins near Schenley, at original railroad milepost 30 north of the former Schenley distillery, now the Schenley Industrial Park. At the yellow trail gate, the trail surface becomes rough gravel to Godfrey (mile 32). The Schenley distillery bottle dump is at Aladdin, between Schenley and Godfrey. At Godfrey the railbed is divided by a post-and-wire fence between the trail and the access road for a long series of summer cottages, camps, and trailers. Camps continue through Kelly (mile 34.8) to Lock and Dam 6 (mile 35.3; the lock is on the other side of the river) on the Allegheny River.

At Kelly a bait shop sells ice, pop, and snacks. The road widens here to provide access to more summer camps, a handicapped-access fishing area, and the power generating plant at Dam 6. From this dam to Logansport (mile 37) and on to Crooked Ck (mile 39), the ballast has been removed from the trail, which improves the ride a little. Logansport features the remains of the original Schenley distillery, most notably the smokestack and water tower. This distillery was active in the 1930s and was replaced by the one at Schenley. The trail crosses Crooked Creek at mile 39 and emerges at a Pa Fish Commission boat launch and parking area in Rosston, south of Ford City. The trail continues to Ford City on the railbed parallel to the road.

From Ford City to Kittanning the trail goes through commercial, industrial, and residential areas with a few interruptions. In Kittanning the trail is marked with a Rails-to-Trails sign where it crosses Market St. From here it continues parallel to the road until it reaches the mouth of Cowanshannock Ck at Gosford (mile 47.2). Here the main road swings away and the trail parallels a dirt road to Mosgrove, at the mouth of Pine Ck (mile 49.8) and then to Lock and Dam 8 (mile 51.5).

About two miles farther along, the trail reaches the edge of the Harbison-Walker Brick Plant, which closed about 1987. The fence that encloses the brick plant blocks the trail. An alternate route follows the road around the other side of the brick plant to the ball field and picnic shelter north of the brick plant in Templeton (mile 54). Supplies are available at Lasher Mercantile, visible across the park from the picnic shelter.

From Templeton the trail continues, still with a rough surface including loose cinders and occasional mudholes, crossing the Mahoning Ck (mile 55) and Red Bank Ck (mile 63.1). On the north side of Red Bank Ck a spur goes east 4 miles to Lawsonham. A mile past Red Bank Ck the main trail bears right to Philipston Tunnel and a spur bears left 2 miles to East Brady. The main trail goes through the tunnel and on to Upper Hillville. However, the tunnel is not yet suitable for use and the trail is not completely clear.

Armstrong Trail	
Location	Along east bank of Allegheny River in Gilpin, Bethel, Manor, Rayburn, Boggs, Pine, Madison Townships in Armstrong County; Brady, Madison, Toby Townships in Clarion County
Trailheads	Schenley, Rosston, Lawsonham, East Brady
Length, Surface	About 52 miles; primitive
Character	Access road for river and summer homes
Usage restrictions	Horses ok while trail is still primitive; no motorized vehicles; no snowmobiles
Amenities	Occasional groceries; swimming in river
Driving time from Pittsburgh	1 hour north-north-east

Local history, attractions

The railroad was most recently part of the Consolidated Rail Corporation (Conrail) system. Prior to that the tracks belonged to the Penn Central Railroad.

River navigation was initiated here by the construction of the Kittanning Feeder of the Pennsylvania Main Line Canal in the early 19th century. This 14-mile extension connected Kittanning with the main stem of the canal at Freeport.

Development plans

When Conrail decided to sell the 52.5-mile corridor, the Armstrong County Conservancy acquired it through the Allegheny Valley Land Trust. The trail was dedicated in June 1992. Rails and ties have been removed. Planned improvements include brush cutting, signage, trash removal, drainage repairs, barriers to motorized vehicles, rail and tie removal, bridge and tunnel safety upgrades, and eventual installation of a packed crushed limestone surface.

The Allegheny Valley Land Trust has been selling the railbed ballast to PennDoT. In the sections where the ballast has been harvested (e.g, south of Rosston), the trail surface is noticeably improved, though still rough.

By 1995, a great deal of the trail was suitable for mountain bikes. Although the trail is unfinished and often rough, we include it here because of its potential role as a link in the Pittsburgh-Erie connection.

Access points

In the interest of good relations with trail neighbors, the trail association requests that you park only in designated parking lots. These include the Fish Commission parking lots in Rosston and Templeton, the B.C. Snyder Picnic Area north of Kittanning, and the trail lots at East Brady and Lawsonham.

Vicinity: Directions begin at the intersection of PA66, PA28/US422, and two local streets just south of Kittanning. To reach this point from Pittsburgh, go northeast on PA28; after PA28/US422 crosses the Allegheny River, it swings north and meets PA66 at a traffic light as PA28/US422 changes from freeway to uncontrolled road.

Except for Ford City/Rosston, the B.C. Snyder Picnic area, and East Brady, these trailheads are fairly inaccessible. Take a good map as well as these directions.

South trailhead (Schenley): From the PA28/US422/PA66 intersection, go south on PA66 for about 13 miles to SR2062 (Schenley Rd). Turn west (right) on SR2062 and continue about 4 miles to Schenley. Before crossing the tracks to the Post Office, turn right and continue upstream on the land side of the tracks to the aqua Eljer warehouse. Follow the road across the tracks here and continue a little farther to parking near the gate. To get to Schenley, you have to *really want* to get to Schenley.

Ford City/Rosston trailhead: From the PA28/US422/PA66 intersection, go south (left) on SR2011 (it will be called Hill St in McGrann and 4th Av in Ford City) for about 3 miles, where you will merge with PA128. Follow PA128 until it turns right to cross the Allegheny River. Instead of crossing the Allegheny, go straight on Ross Av between the tracks and the river. Continue 1 mile to the Pa Fish Commission boat launching area just after Rosston and just before the trail crosses Crooked Creek.

B.C. Snyder Picnic Area trailhead: From the PA28/US422/PA66 intersection, go north on South Water St through Kittanning (the road becomes SR1033) for about 4 miles. The picnic area is at the mouth of Cowanshannock Ck.

Templeton trailhead: There's public parking at the Pa Fish Commission access area in Templeton. It's 8-10 miles on winding local roads from the nearest main road. If you want to get to Templeton, take a good map. It may be shorter to get there by trail from the B. C. Snyder area (7 miles up the trail) than it is to drive there.

Lawsonham trailhead: From the PA28/US422/PA66 intersection, follow the instructions below to pass through East Brady on PA68. Continue east on PA68. At New Athens, turn right (south) on TR880 (Henry Rd) toward Lawsonham. Turn left on TR456 (Pinoak

Rd) and follow it to the end. The parking lot is to the left at the bottom of a long hill sloping to the right. The trail goes down Redbank Creek to the west of the parking lot.

East Brady trailhead: From the PA28/US422/PA66 intersection, go north on South Water St into Kittanning. Cross the Allegheny River on the bridge at Market St. At the end of the bridge, turn left on Pine Hill Rd and follow Pine Hill Rd until it joins PA268. Follow PA268 north for about 16 miles to Kepples Corners and turn east (right) on PA68. Follow PA68 about 8 miles, back across the Allegheny River, to East Brady PA68 is called Third St in East Brady. In East Brady, turn right on Grant St, go 3 blocks, and turn left on Sixth St. Continue on Sixth St to the brown tarpaper brick covered garage. Just past this garage, turn right and follow the alley through the park, but not as far as the tennis court. The parking lot is at the bottom of the hill along the old railroad bed. To reach the trail from the parking lot, walk up the parking lot exit road, turn right on the dirt road down hill. After passing a number of campsites and going over a small bridge over a gully, this road eventually joins the old railroad bed.

Amenities

Rest rooms, water: None

Bike shop, rental: None known

Restaurant, groceries: Restaurants in Kittanning and Ford City. Groceries or snacks also at Kelly, Rosston (Coleman Marina), and Templeton (Lasher Mercantile).

Camping, simple lodging: None known

Swimming, fishing: Trail runs along the Allegheny River. Swimming is unsupervised; be especially careful when the water is high. Do not trespass to get to the river.

Winter sports: Cross-country skiing. No snowmobiles.

Trail organization

Norman Karp, President
Armstrong Rails-to-Trails Association
222 Market St
Kittanning PA 16201
(412) 543-4478

Membership: $10/year individual or family

Maps, guides, other references

USGS Topographic Maps: Freeport, Leechburg, Kittanning, Mosgrove, Templeton, East Brady, Rimersburg.

Great Shamokin Path

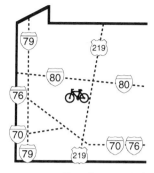

Along Cowanshannock Creek from Rose Valley to NuMine in Armstrong County

Both the Great Shamokin Path and PA85 run alongside Cowanshannock Ck, the rail-trail on the south side and the road on the north. The trail connects two lakes, Devils Washbasin in the west and White Lake/Wetland to the east. The creek is well wooded, so aside from some road noise, the trail feels isolated. The surface is packed fine gravel, often with grass growing. It is generally about 20 feet wide, but in many places grass grows knee-high on the edges and the open path is just about wide enough for two bikes to ride abreast. The trail properly gated and posted against motorized vehicles (but only that—we didn't see any specific identification as the Great Shamokin Path).

The trail follows the route of its namesake, a traditional Indian path that connected the Susquehanna River basin with Kittanning. In this area the Great Shamokin Path followed Cowanshannock Ck. It's a pleasant, though short, ride through woods and small farms with frequent glimpses of the creek. Small wildlife is abundant: On one trip we saw chipmunks, rabbits, a groundhog, ducks, kingfishers, and a wild turkey; many other birds made a constant chirping chatter. You'll also pass a fish hatchery. One small development appears to have been built as a company town; the originally-identical houses have acquired individual identities over the years.

It's about three miles from Yatesboro, near Rose Valley, to NuMine near the east end. If you go west from the Yatesboro access path, in about 0.3 miles a pile of I-beams in the trail will warn you that the bridge piers immediately ahead are missing their bridge. This is, at least for now, the end of the line. From the NuMine access, another 0.7 miles brings you to White Lake.

Great Shamokin Path	
Location	Near Yatesboro, Cowanshannock Township, Armstrong County
Trailheads	Yatesboro, Rural Valley, Meredith, NuMine
Length, Surface	4 miles; fine packed gravel, often with grass
Character	Little-used, rural, shady, flat
Usage restrictions	Horses ok; no motorized vehicles
Amenities	Latrine
Driving time from Pittsburgh	1 hour east-northeast

Extensions of the ride

The ride can be extended in two ways: westward from the Yatesboro parking area and northward into the four small towns that lie just north of PA85. Both extensions are open to motor vehicles, but you shouldn't find very much traffic, and it won't be fast.

Westward: When you reach the missing bridge that now terminates the trail, retrace your steps 0.3 miles to the intersection with the path to Yatesboro. Turn north on the path, crossing Cowanshannock creek and emerging on PA85. Without crossing PA85, walk west (against traffic) about 30 feet on the shoulder and turn left (south) on the abandoned railroad right-of-way. The surface is much like the rail-trail, but it now runs through open farms rather than woods. This section is open to traffic, but it appears unlikely that you will encounter any (in part because a small bridge has partly fallen in). This segment continues 1.2 miles to a large bridge with ties but no deck. It's not worth going beyond this bridge; the trail deteriorates over the next quarter mile and eventually disappears into backyards and weeds.

Northward: From the Yatesboro parking area, you can follow the former railroad roadbed (the one described in the previous paragraph) north across PA85 and up the valley. After it bends to the north it gets pretty well grown up, and we quit after about 0.7 mile and came back down the paved road. You can also follow footpaths just north of PA85 into Yatesboro. This will put you on Main St. At the post office, jog over a block (you'll recognize the former railroad station) and follow the back street, which carries very little traffic, until it ends in a group of gravel driveways in Rural Valley. At that point, backtrack a couple of blocks to the main cross street (Water St), turn south, cross PA85 and Cowanshannock Creek, and return via the rail-trail.

Access points

Vicinity: Directions begin as you approach Yatesboro headed east on PA85. To reach this point from Pittsburgh, go north on PA28 through Kittanning. Follow PA28/66 north about 1.5 miles to PA85. Turn right (east) on PA85. You reach the Yatesboro turn-off in about 8 miles, NuMine in about 11.

West trailhead: On PA85 the Valley Village Store marks the west edge of Yatesboro. Just east of the store, the road surface shows where the railroad was removed. Just past that point and just before the turnoff to Yatesboro, there is an unmarked parking area for about 4 cars on the right. A rideable path leads south from the parking area, across Cowanshannock Creek to the trail crossing. Beware of loose gravel as you descend from PA85 to the bridge.

East trailhead: On PA85, go about 3 miles east from Yatesboro. Turn south (right) at the intersection where you would turn north (left) to go to NuMine. Immediately cross Cowanshannock Creek, then turn right between the ballfield and the creek. You will soon see the gated trailhead. This is the easier end to identify. You can drive in a little farther to the White Lake picnic area.

Other access: Two other roads crossing PA85 are marked to turn north to Rural Valley and Meredith. If you turn south at either of these intersections you will quickly cross first Cowanshannock Creek and then the trail.

Amenities

Rest rooms, water: Latrine at ballfield near east trailhead; rest rooms at ballfield in Rural Valley. No water, except at stores and restaurants.

Bike shop, rentals: None, but there's a hardware store in Rural Valley.

Restaurant, groceries: Rural Valley has a drug store, grocery, pizza shop, and several bars, all on Main St. We had a good dinner at Charley's Place. Valley Village Store on PA85 west of Yatesboro.

Camping, simple lodging: None

Swimming, fishing: Unsupervised swimming in the creek, if it's high enough.

Winter sports: Cross-country skiing.

Trail organization

Pam Meade, President
Cowanshannock Creek Watershed Association
PO Box 307
Rural Valley PA 16249-0307
(412) 783-6692
Membership: $3.00/year individual

Maps, guides, other references

USGS Topographic Maps: Rural Valley.

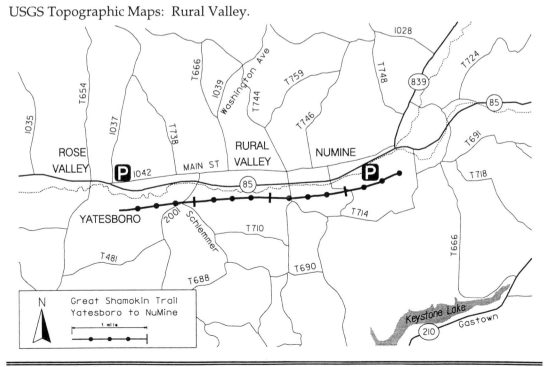

Roaring Run Trail

Southeast of Apollo in Armstrong County

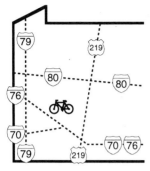

Roaring Run Trail parallels the Kiskiminetas River from Cherry Lane southeast of Apollo upstream for 3.7 miles toward (but not nearly to) Edmon. The surface is finished as a 10-foot packed limestone path for 1.6 miles to the mouth of Roaring Run. After crossing Roaring Run, the trail progressively deteriorates as it approaches the Brownstown Mine (which is private property beyond the end of the trail). It's evident that development is underway, though, as the drainage has been improved. At present, there is only one trailhead, so plan a round-trip in and out.

Most recently, this corridor served as the route of the Pennsylvania Railroad Apollo industrial extension track. Before that, though, it was the towpath for a section of the Pennsylvania Main Line Canal. Survey stones and other remains from the canal era can still be found along the trail. An interpretive sign near the trailhead explains the workings of the canal. The easiest survey stones to find are near this sign.

The trail begins at a parking lot at the end of a small residential community. There's a picnic table here, and several benches dot the trail. As you head upstream, eastbound from the parking lot, you'll soon pass Milepost 1. Shortly thereafter you enter the woods, with frequent views of the Kiskiminetas River.

Roaring Run Trail	
Location	Southeast of Apollo, Kiskiminetas Township, Armstrong County
Trailheads	Apollo (no access at other end)
Length, Surface	3.7 miles, 1.6 finished in packed limestone
Character	Open shade along river
Usage restrictions	No motorized vehicles; no horses
Amenities	Fishing
Driving time from Pittsburgh	45 minutes north-east

Near mile 1.5 you can still see the remains of Lock 15 of the Pennsylvania Main Line Canal and its associated dam, which was originally 16 feet high. The lock was also numbered #2 on the Kiskiminetas River. Here a "guard lock" moved barge traffic from the canal downstream to the 4-mile pool created by the dam. Upstream from the dam, the canal boats used the slackwater pool of the river instead of a separate canal prism. Mules used the riverbank as a towpath. A lock house and inn were also located near the mouth of Roaring Run.

Long a victim of industrial pollution, especially mine runoff, the Kiskiminetas River is making a comeback. You'll find good fishing at milepost 2 and at a big hole near the mouth of Roaring Run.

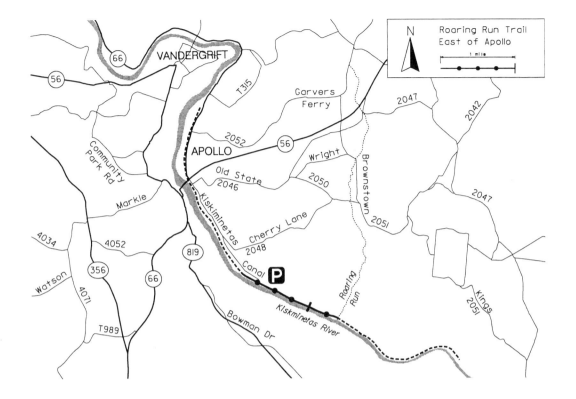

The current end of the finished trail is at the bridge over Roaring Run. The area is open for hunting, so exercise caution during hunting seasons.

Local history, attractions

The former Pennsylvania Main Line Canal connected Philadelphia with Pittsburgh with three canals, a railroad, and the Allegheny Portage Railway, a combination railroad and inclined plane. The Western Division ran from Johnstown down the Conemaugh, Kiskiminetas, and Allegheny Rivers to Pittsburgh. Many traces of the canal can still be found along the trail. The Roaring Run Watershed Association is identifying and marking these traces and is in the process of documenting the canal remains in Armstrong County for the National Register of Historic Places. The RRWA holds numerous events along this trail; many include historical interpretation of these remains. The Lower Trail, along the Frankstown Branch of the Juniata River, runs along the Juniata Division of the Pennsylvania Main Line Canal.

Extensions of the ride

It's possible to add 1.3 miles to the trip by parking in Apollo and riding on Kiskiminetas Ave parallel to the river (follow the driving directions to the trailhead).

Mountain bikers may ride up alongside Roaring Run on a very rough dirt road. If you start on the west side of the mouth of Roaring Run (the side closer to Apollo) you'll ford the creek once; if you start on the east side you'll ford it twice. This dirt road climbs vigorously along the creek for a bit over a mile through Roaring Run Watershed Association's new parcel. As the road leaves the creek it enters private property; turn around here and enjoy the ride back. Along the way you'll pass Rock Furnace, one of the first iron furnaces in Western Pennsylvania. It was a "tea-kettle" furnace that operated from 1825 to 1855. In operation, it depended on charcoal, limestone, and iron ore from the adjacent hills. A model is on display at the Historical Society museum in Tarentum.

Development plans

The Roaring Run Watershed Association is working to protect the entire watershed of Roaring Run. They are working to extend the trail along Roaring Run to Brownstown Road and (eventually) upstream along the Kiskiminetas River to Edmon. They have regular volunteer activities to maintain the trail and develop amenities.

The Kovalchick family donated the initial trail segment, from the trail-head parking lot to its end 3.5 miles upstream along the Kiskiminetas River. Current activities focus on securing additional acreage in the watersheds of Rattling Run and Roaring Run and on completing half a mile of trail eastward from the Roaring Run bridge.

Access points

Vicinity: Directions begin on PA66 northbound across the Kiskiminetas River entering Apollo. To reach this point from Pittsburgh, take US22 east to PA286 and PA286 to PA380. Go north on PA380 to PA66. Go north on PA66 to Apollo.

Apollo trailhead (the only one): After crossing the Kiskiminetas River on PA66, turn right at the first stop light onto Kiskiminetas Av. Follow this road through town to Cherry Lane. About 1 mile from the stop light take the right fork into Canal Rd instead of going up the hill. The road dead-ends in the trailhead parking lot 1.3 miles from the traffic light in Apollo.

Amenities

Rest rooms, water: None

Bike shop, rentals: None, though you can get basic hardware at the True Value Hardware or the Ben Franklin store in Apollo.

Restaurant, groceries: Within sight of the traffic light in Apollo you'll find Patrick's Pub (try the pizza and wings), a CoGo's, a Subway, and an IGA Grocery.

Camping, simple lodging: None

Swimming, fishing: The Kiskiminetas River is right next to the trail. There's good fishing at milepost 2 and the big hole at the mouth of Roaring Run (near the trail bridge).

Fisherfolk report bass, catfish, drum, suckers, etc. The river often has swift currents and deep holes, and the trail managers discourage swimming.

Trail organization

Andy Schreffler, President
Roaring Run Watershed Association
PO Box 40
Spring Church PA 15686
(412) 568-1483
Membership $5/year individual, $15.00/year family

Maps, guides, other references

USGS Topographic Maps: Vandergrift.

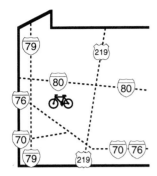

Butler-Freeport Community Trail

Along Little Buffalo Creek from Freeport in Armstrong County to Butler in Butler County

In using this trail, you should be aware that some nearby land-owners question the trail operator's title to the trail and right to use the land. As of January 1996, this disagreement is being litigated. In addition, some sections of the trail may be obstructed or posted. We recommend against trespassing or antagonizing trail neighbors anywhere, but especially so here. Since the status of this matter changes from time to time, you may wish to check with the trail operator about the current status.

The Butler-Freeport Trail is planned to follow 20 miles of the former Butler Branch Rail Line of Conrail. The planned route runs from Freeport Borough, along Buffalo and Little Buffalo Creeks to Great Belt, then down Coal Run to Butler. It passes through wooded areas, open farmland, small villages, and deep valleys. Buffalo Creek is on the registry of Scenic Waterways. It's well sheltered in a shaded valley. The trail is nearly flat, but as rail-trails go the gradient is somewhat more noticeable than usual. At present, the middle 11.5 miles have been surfaced. The 8-foot wide trail is finished in crushed limestone. Benches are liberally sprinkled along the trail, especially between Sandy Lick and Cabot. A few original railroad mileposts remain; they appear to count mileage from Laneville. An initial segment from Sarver to Cabot was officially opened in fall 1992. In 1994 this was rebuilt and extended to run 11.5 miles from south of Sandy Lick to Herman.

The southern end of the finished trail starts just north of an unfinished trestle near Monroe (no road access). From here to Sandy Lick (Bear Creek Rd) it runs on a narrow bench between the cliff and Little Buffalo Creek. 1.2 miles north of Sandy Lick the trail passes a lovely home set on a small lake. The creek is almost always within view or at least within hearing—the trail crosses it four times between Sarver and Cabot, and as a bonus it also crosses a small unnamed creek. 1.9 miles north of Sarver there are traces of an old industrial site on the west side of the trail. This is the first, and the most conspicuous, of several such ruins. They are part of the processing plants for the Franklin Glass and Ford Glass quarries. Foundations and walls appear on both sides of the trail for the next half-mile or so, and the remnants of two stone or concrete dams are visible in the creek on the northeast side. As the trail approaches Cabot, a series of beaver dams pool up the creek; cat-tails mark another wetland 0.8 mile north of Cabot.

North of Cabot there are more signs of development, with small towns, parallel roads, businesses, and farms. The power substation 0.8 mile south of Great Belt was once the site of the world's then-largest oil storage facility. The railroad cut near the substation marks the end of the long climb. From here to Herman the trail goes traverses cuts and fills on top of the ridge. For now, the trail effectively stops at Herman, where the bridge is unfinished and blocked. The intersection is dominated by St. Fidelius School, founded 1877. An additional 3/4 mile of trail extends beyond the gap, but it is not accessible

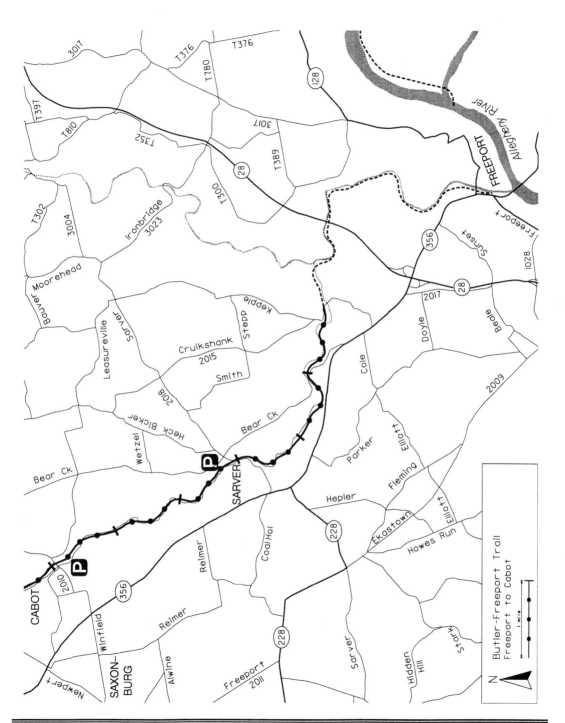

from here. The other end of this segment emerges near the Summit Township municipal building, 0.25 miles west on Herman Rd, then 0.5 miles west on Bonnie Brook Rd.

Butler-Freeport Community Trail	
Location	Buffalo, Winfield, Jefferson, and Summit Townships, Butler County; South Buffalo Township, Armstrong County
Trailheads	Sarver, Cabot, Herman, eventually Laneville, Butler
Length, Surface	11.75 miles developed, 21 miles planned; crushed limestone
Character	Uncrowded, wooded, shady, flat
Usage restrictions	Horses ok alongside improved trail; no motorized vehicles
Amenities	Food
Driving time from Pittsburgh	45 minutes north-east

Local history, attractions

The trail follows the right-of-way of the former Butler Branch line of the Western Pennsylvania Railroad (more recently Conrail). This was the first railroad built in Butler county. It was completed in 1871 to provide freight and passenger service to Butler. The villages along the trail were built to serve the railroad, which ran as many as six passenger trains a day.

Valley Mill is just down the street from the Laneville trailhead. A similar flour mill is open to the public in McConnells Mill State Park. Cooper Cabin, a restored log cabin, is open Sundays in the summer. It is 0.3 miles west of Cabot; follow the signs. Historic Saxonburg is an old German settler village with shops, restaurants, and a museum. It is 2 miles west of Cabot.

Development plans

Several passenger stations once adjoined the trail. The trail council hopes to rebuild the one in Cabot. The bridge at Herman is scheduled to be rebuilt.

Plans call for the trail to eventually begin at Laneville, the section of Freeport west of Buffalo Ck. The 4.8-mile segment from Laneville to the current start near Monroe is not officially open yet. At present its surface is raw ballast, and it includes two unfinished bridges. The area once supported numerous clay mines and the area is littered with specialty bricks. A large area of industrial ruins, which we call Kiva Town Center, is in the flats on the west side of the trail about 2 miles north of Laneville (just north of the handsome dressed-brick culvert). This is the remnant of the Harbison Brick Co brickworks; it's private property. The round kiva-like structures were kilns; five of these domed brick kilns baked bricks at a temperature of 2000°. At the cliff about 1/4 mile south of Winfield Junction, the undersides of overhanging rocks show fossils and drill holes left over from railroad construction.

North of Herman, the trail is eventually planned to continue for 4 miles from the municipal building at Bonnie Brook Rd down Coal Run to near Connoquenessing Creek

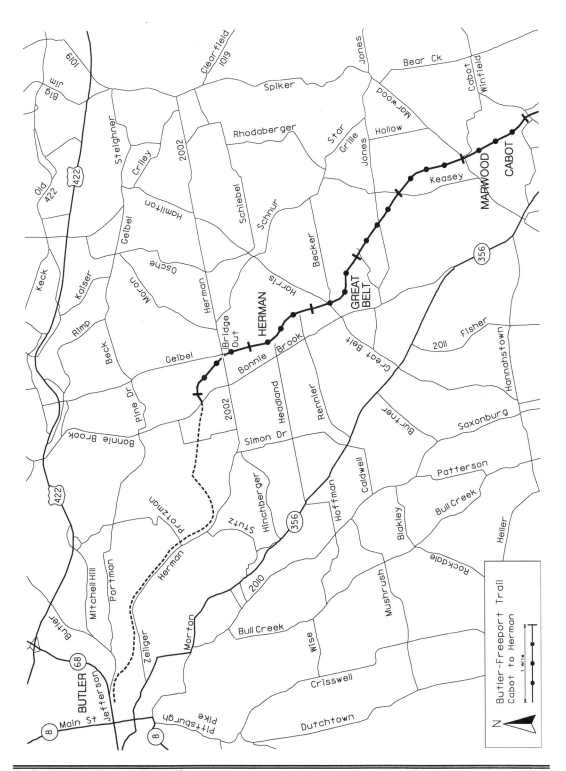

Butler-Freeport Trail
Cabot to Herman

N

in Butler. This will be only about 6-8 miles from Moraine State Park. Butler County is considering a network of bike trails that may close this gap.

Access points

Vicinity for northern trailheads: Directions begin on PA356 headed north from PA28 (except for Laneville, which begins eastbound on PA356). To reach this point from Pittsburgh, go northeast on PA28 to Exit 17 (the second Freeport exit). This is about 20 miles northeast of the Highland Park Bridge interchange on PA 28.

Sarver trailhead: Follow PA356 3.6 miles north from PA28. Turn right (northeast) on Sarver Rd (SR2018). Go down the hill and along the creek for 0.8 mile. Just after crossing the creek and passing the volunteer fire department, turn left into the parking area alongside the trail.

Cabot trailhead: Follow PA356 6.5 miles north from PA28. Turn right (northeast) on Winfield-Cabot Rd (SR2010) at the traffic light in Knox Chapel. The trail crosses this road about half a mile later, in Cabot.

Amenities

Rest rooms, water: Rest rooms in restaurants for patrons.

Bike shop, rental: None at present.

Restaurant, groceries: In Cabot, Cabot Country Inn is a neighborhood bar with a hamburger-type menu. Dottie's Market is a minimal market, but it's connected to the Fox's Pizza Den, which serves hamburgers and sandwiches as well as pizza. There are several restaurants in Knox Chapel, on PA356 0.5 mile west of Cabot.

Camping, simple lodging: Smith Grove Campground 1.5 miles east of trail at Herman. Hotel and Bed-and-Breakfast in Saxonburg 3 miles west of trail at Cabot.

Swimming, fishing: You might be able to swim in the creek, if it has enough water. But in the seasons when you'd want to be swimming the creek is probably almost dry. The trail council does not promote swimming. No fishing near trail.

Winter sports: The trail is protected from the sun, so XC skiing is good. No snowmobiles.

Trail organizations

Ron Bennett	Buffalo Township
Butler-Freeport Comm. Trail Council	109 Bear Creek Rd
PO Box 533	Sarver PA 16055
Saxonburg PA 16056-0533	
(412) 352-4783	(412) 295-2648

Membership $10/year individual, $15/year family

Maps, guides, other references

USGS Topographic Maps: Freeport, Curtisville, Saxonburg, Butler.

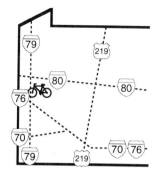

Moraine State Park (Lake Arthur)

Bicycle concession at North Shore Drive to Marina Restaurant, Moraine State Park in Butler County

The designated bicycle trail runs on the north side of Lake Arthur, generally between North Shore Drive and the lake. It winds in and out of trees, up and down gentle hills, past picnic areas and other park activities and facilities. The trail passes several boat launching areas and provides views of the sailing and other boating activities on the lake. The swimming area for this side of the lake is near the trail (miles 3.6-3.8). The east end (mile 7.2) is at the Marina Restaurant. The park is very popular, so you'll have plenty of company any time during the season.

The route of the trail is lovely. Unfortunately, the surface itself is very narrow (only 7') and the asphalt is often rough. Sharp curves and short steep dips make the trail interesting. However, sight lines are quite short, and it's usually busy. If this trail had a smooth 12' path, it would be a gem.

Moraine State Park Bike Trail	
Location	Moraine State Park, Worth Township, Butler County
Trailheads	Bicycle concession, Lakeview Beach area, Marina restaurant
Length, Surface	7.2 miles; fair asphalt 7' wide
Character	Busy, park setting, mostly sunny, gentle hills, sharp curves, steep dips
Usage restrictions	Snowmobiles ok; no motorized vehicles; no horses
Amenities	Rest rooms, water, bike rental, food, swimming, fishing
Driving time from Pittsburgh	1 hour north

Local history, attractions

During the ice age 14,000 years ago, the Wisconsin Ice Sheet came just this far south, where it dammed Muddy Creek to create a large glacial lake. When the glacier receded the lake burst, and the water it liberated carved the deep gorge a few miles west on Slippery Rock Creek, making major changes to the regional drainage patterns. Geological remnants of glaciation, including the moraine and an esker can still be found in the area. Present-day Lake Arthur is in approximately the same location as the glacial lake.

More recently, this area has been exploited for its minerals: first oil in the late 19th century, then coal. Deep mines predominated in the early 20th century, and the area was strip-mined in the 1940s and 1950s.

A park was proposed in 1951 when a geological survey revealed traces of the glacial lake. Extensive restoration was required to reclaim the land that is now the park. Deep mines were sealed, hundreds of oil and gas wells were plugged, and strip mines were re-contoured. The park opened in 1970.

Extensions of the ride

A 7.2-mile mountain bike trail lies east of the Davis Hollow Marina. This includes very steep rocky sections and is definitely not a novice trail. It's not our kind of riding, and it's mentioned here only because it's handy. From the Marina Restaurant, follow the road out to North Shore Drive, turn right and go to the very end of the parking lot at the marina. The trailhead is the other side of the canoe racks. You can reach another trail-head by taking Mt Union Rd north from North Shore Drive where the road to Nealy's Point goes south. This trailhead is about a third of a mile up Mt Union, just past the Glacier Ridge Hiking Trail trailhead.

Access points

Vicinity: Directions begin on either US422 or I79 headed toward Moraine State Park. Details depend on where you're coming from.

West Trailhead (bicycle rental concession):

> *From the east:* You'll approach the park headed west on US422. About a mile after you cross the lake (and just before the I79 intersection), take the "North Shore" exit from US422. Go a quarter-mile to the stop/yield signs. Turn right and follow signs for 0.8 mile to the bicycle concession and trailhead parking.

> *From the south:* You'll approach the park headed north on I79. Take the PA488 exit (Portersville, Exit 28) and go west 0.6 miles to US19 in Portersville. Turn north (right) on US19, go 0.5 miles, and turn right on SR4007 (West Park Rd, also num-bered TR890). Follow signs for "North Shore Moraine State Park". Go 2.8 miles on SR4007, crossing I79, US422, and Muddy Creek. Just after crossing the creek, turn right and follow signs 0.8 mile to the bicycle concession and trailhead parking.

> *From the west:* You'll approach the park headed east on US422. Turn south (right) on US19, go a bit over half a mile to Burnside Rd and turn left. Follow Burnside Rd just over a mile to SR4007 (West Park Rd) and turn left. Go 0.5 mile on SR4007, crossing US422 and a creek. Just after the creek crossing, turn right and follow signs 0.8 mile to the bicycle concession and trailhead parking.

> *From the north:* You'll approach the park headed south on I79. Take the US422 exit (Exit 29). Go west 1.2 miles to US19, turn south (left) on US19, then proceed as if you were coming from the west.

East trailhead (Marina restaurant): Instead of turning into West trailhead (bicycle conces-sion) parking, continue on the access road, which becomes North Shore Dr. Follow signs to the Marina Restaurant.

Other access: Since the trail lies between North Shore Drive and the lake, practically any parking lot along North Shore drive provides access, especially the ones at lakeside.

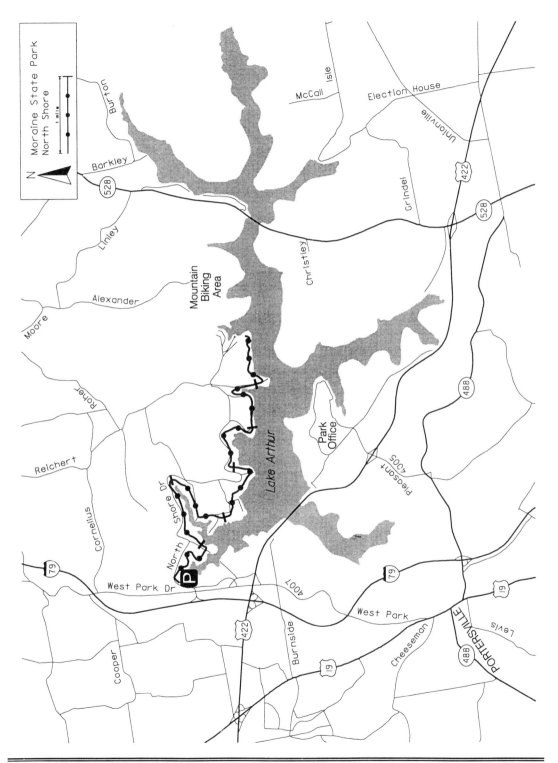

Amenities

Rest rooms, water: Water and rest rooms are available at both trailheads and at the Lakeview Picnic area and the Watts Bay Marina in between. There are also water fountains at intervals.

Bike shop, rentals: No bike shop, but a rental concession operates at the west trailhead daily from Memorial Day to Labor Day and warm weekends in April, May, September, and October.

Restaurant, groceries: The Marina Restaurant serves full meals during the season. There's a snack bar near Lakeview Beach, near milepost 3.7. The bike rental concession has vending machines.

Camping, simple lodging: No camping in the park. The park office can give you a list of private campgrounds and hotels in the area.

Swimming, fishing: Swimming in the state park is permitted only at official swimming areas; they issue citations to swimmers at other locations. The north shore swimming area is at Lakeview, near milepost 3.7. It's open Memorial Day to Labor Day. Fishing in the lake features muskellunge, northern pike, striper, largemouth bass, walleye, channel catfish, black crappie, and bluegill.

Winter sports: The cross-country skiing area is quite short and on the south side of the lake. Jennings Nature Reserve, not far northeast, has a more extensive trail system suitable for cross-country skiing. The bike trail becomes part of the snowmobile trail in the winter. There's also ice fishing, ice boating, ice skating, and sledding.

Trail organization

PA Department of Environmental Resources
Moraine State Park
RD 1, Box 212
Portersville PA 16051
(412) 368-8811

Maps, guides, other references

The map in the park's information brochure shows the bike route. Trail maps for the mountain bike area are available at the Park office and the bike rental concession.

USGS Topographic Maps: Portersville, Prospect.

Trails West: Lake Erie and Eastern Ohio

In this section we present several trails on the north and west edges of Pennsylvania -- but not in the Allegheny River watershed. One in on the PA/OH state line; one is on a peninsula in Lake Erie; three are near Cleveland, in northeastern Ohio.

Eastern Ohio isn't western Pennsylvania, but these trails are close at hand, and they're too good to pass up. From Pittsburgh, the Akron-Cleveland area is about as convenient as the Franklin-Oil City area and much closer than Presque Isle. From northwestern Pennsylvania, these trails are closer than the Youghiogheny-Allegheny Highlands system. So we decided that opportunity and convenience are more important than details of geography, and here they are.

All but one of these trails are developed and maintained by public organizations -- state or regional park districts or the National Park Service. Stavich Trail is maintained privately.

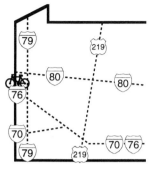

Stavich Bicycle Trail

New Castle PA to Struthers OH in Lawrence County PA and Mahoning County OH

An excellent 8-foot asphalt surface (measured as 9.75 ft) carries you through farmland and woods along the Mahoning River. The trail corridor originally served as railbed for the Penn-Ohio interurban trolley line rather than a railroad. Trolleys are more forgiving about gradients than railroads, so you'll find noticeable (but still slight) slopes. The only scenic drawback is the existing trackage of the Pennsylvania and Lake Erie railroad, especially the switch yard near Struthers. Much of this track is now being salvaged, though two tracks are still in use.

Most of the trail runs through woods and farms with occasional houses near the trail. Just past mile 2 (we use westbound mileposts here), a beaver dam between the trail and the railroad has created a lake and marsh on the opposite side of the trail. At mile 6.9 the trail crosses into Ohio. Ducks sometimes occupy the pond at mile 7.1.

From miles 7.5 to 8.0, the trail is on Liberty St in Lowellville, affording an opportunity for lunch in the parklet on the opposite side of the railroad, across from City Hall. You can buy subs at Ross' Market on Liberty St, a block west of the parklet. Although this short stretch is on roads, traffic is very light and slow.

The trail is largely exposed, making it a good bet for early and late in the season, but a real oven in the summer. Wildflower displays in season are very fine, especially where the edges of the trail have not been mowed. You'll probably meet several others, but the trail is not crowded. A dozen and a half benches and picnic tables have been installed between New Castle and Lowellville, mostly in the four miles nearest New Castle.

Stavich Bicycle Trail	
Location	New Castle PA to Struthers OH, Union and Mahoning Townships in Lawrence County PA; Lowellville and Poland Townships in Mahoning County OH
Trailheads	New Castle PA, Edinburg PA, Lowellville OH, Struthers OH
Length, Surface	12 miles reported, 9.8 measured; asphalt, 8 feet wide (9.75 measured)
Character	Busy, rural, sunny, flat
Usage restrictions	No motorized vehicles; no horses
Amenities	Water, food
Driving time from Pittsburgh	1 hour 10 minutes northwest

Local history, attractions

The trail runs on the path of the former interurban streetcar line that joined Youngstown and New Castle. The John and George Stavich families, together with other local individuals, have taken full responsibility for its development and maintenance. It is one of the earliest rail-trails, having been dedicated in June 1983 and improved over time.

The Pennsylvania and Ohio Canal, also known as the "Cross-Cut" Canal, connected the Beaver and Erie Division of the Pennsylvania Main Line Canal with the Ohio and Erie Canal in Ohio. It started at New Castle and ran west on the Mahoning River to Youngstown, Warren, and Akron. Operating from 1840 to 1872, it carried primarily pig iron, iron ore, and passengers.

The trail follows also follows the route of the even earlier Mahoning Path, an Indian path that connected Beaver to Cayahaga (now Akron). The Delaware word mahoni means "deer lick". Adding the "-ing" ending makes Mahoning mean "at the deer lick".

Outskirts of Lowellville

Extensions of the ride

A 1.9-mile loop between the trail and the Mahoning River offers a variation on the route. This road is named East River Rd where it crosses the trail at westbound mile 4.2 and Hillsville Rd where it crosses the trail at mile 5.7. You can turn toward the river at either of these crossings; the road name changes where a side road crosses the river.

It's possible to loop from the west end of the trail back to Lowellville on the south side of the Mahoning River. From the west end of the trail, go west 1.1 miles on OH289 (Broad St) and turn left on OH616 (Bridge St) and cross the bridge. Go straight at two lights; a short block after the second light take the left fork on Lowellville Rd, continue along the river to Lowellville, and cross the bridge back into Lowellville. Of this 4.7 miles on roads, two miles have moderate traffic and none has good shoulder.

The ride also can be extended to the west with an excursion to the Bike Nashbar outlet store, about 5 miles away on the south side of Youngstown. From the west trailhead, go

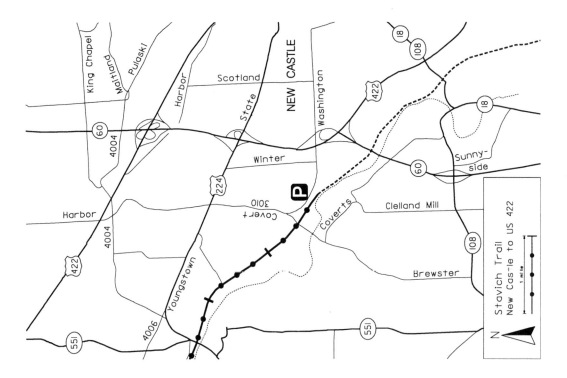

west 1.1 miles on OH289 (Broad St), turn left on OH616 (Bridge St), and cross the bridge. Go straight at the first traffic light, then right on State St at the second traffic light. Take the first left (Poland St), then the first right (Terrace St), then the next left (diagonally onto Elm). Go up Elm St about 0.5 miles and turn right on Garfield. Garfield emerges from the residential district as Midlothian Blvd. You could continue on Midlothian, but there's a lot of traffic. A better plan is to shift right one block to the parallel road, Mt Vernon. Follow Mt Vernon until it ends, go around the barricade, turn right on Loveland, and take the next left on South Heights, which again parallels Midlothian in a residential area. When South Heights ends, go diagonally left through the park, emerging on Midlothian just before it goes under I680. Tough it out on Midlothian for 0.6 miles under I680 and through three traffic lights. Just past the third traffic light (and just past Schwebel's bakery) turn left on Simon. Nashbar is a long block down on the left. (To get there by car, take Exit 9B from I680, go west on Midlothian and proceed as above).

Access points

Vicinity: Directions begin on US224 westbound from its intersection with PA60/US422 in New Castle. To reach this point from Pittsburgh, follow the Parkway West past Pittsburgh International Airport, continuing north on PA60 and paying toll when it becomes PA Toll 60 (the Turnpike extension). 4.7 miles after the exit toll booth, take the US224 west exit (Sampson St) and follow the sign for US224 to Poland.

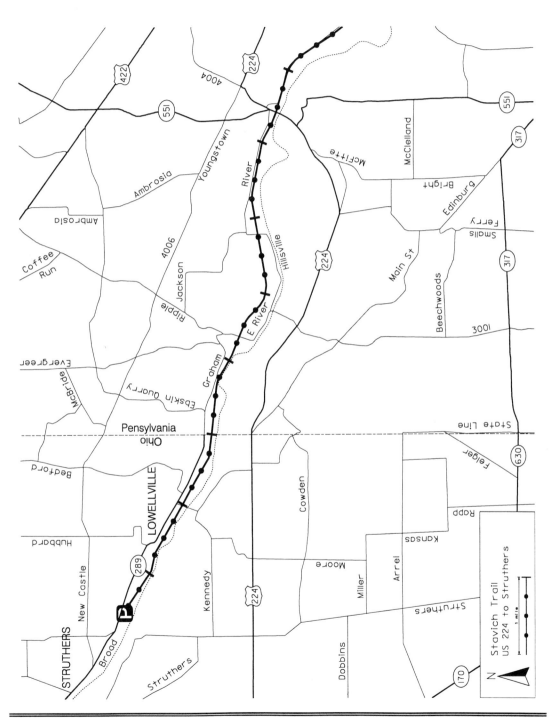

East trailhead (New Castle): 0.7 miles after turning onto US224, turn left on Covert Rd (SR3010) at Riley's and a ballfield. Follow this road 1.4 miles to trailhead parking. *Alternate route:* A shorter but trickier way to get to the New Castle trailhead is to take the PA108 (Mt Jackson, Exit 19) exit from PA Toll 60, go left toward Mt Jackson for 0.5 mile, turn right on Clelland Mill Rd at the crossroads just past Thompson's Alternator/Starter Service (beware—the street sign is hiding in a tree), go 1.4 miles on Clelland Mill Rd, turn left at the fork/triangle onto unmarked Coverts Rd, go 0.8 mile on Coverts Rd, turn right at the "T" intersection of Coverts Rd and Brewster Rd, follow this road for 0.7 mile across a railroad, the Mahoning River, another railroad, and the trail, then at the stop sign turn slightly right onto an unmarked road (West Washington St extension) to the trailhead parking about 0.1 mile ahead.

West trailhead (Struthers): Follow US224 10.5 miles to Poland OH. Turn right (north) on OH616. Follow OH616 across Mahoning River, immediately turn right on OH289 (Broad St), and continue 1.1 miles to trailhead parking.

Amenities

Rest rooms, water: No rest rooms. Seasonal water fountain in park in Lowellville; Ross' Market will fill your water bottle when you get your sandwich.

Bike shop, rentals: None, but Nashbar Outlet Store 5 miles west, in Youngstown OH.

Restaurant, groceries: Restaurants in Lowellville (closed Sundays). Groceries and sub sandwiches at Ross' Market on Liberty St in Lowellville. If you ride the extension to Nashbar, you'll find restaurants at the intersection of Loveland and Midlothian (near the end of Mt Vernon).

Camping, simple lodging: None

Swimming, fishing: In the Mahoning River, in the highly unlikely event that the water quality is up to your (or the fish's) standards.

Winter sports: Cross-country skiing.

Trail organization

> Gary Slaven
> Falcon Foundry
> 6th and Water Sts
> PO Box 301
> Lowellville OH 44436-0301
> (216) 536-6221

Maps, guides, other references

Trail brochure. "Two states on two wheels: the Stavich Bicycle Trail"

USGS Topographic Maps: Bessemer, Edinburg, Youngstown.

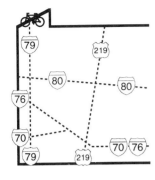

Presque Isle State Park Bikepath

Presque Isle State Park in Erie County

Presque Isle is a 3200 acre peninsula of glacial sand that juts 7 miles into Lake Erie from the city of Erie. A loop road popular with sightseers extends the length of the peninsula. A 5.8-mile paved multipurpose trail roughly parallels this road from the park entrance along the south (inland) side of the peninsula to Perry's Monument. The trail is barely two lanes wide, and it is often crowded.

The first two miles of the trail share the narrow neck of the peninsula with the road and parking lots, though the trail is separated from the road by shrubbery for most of this distance. The next mile or so pass through picnic areas. The last half of the trail skirts the edges of several of the ponds that lace the wide end of the peninsula, usually in view of Presque Isle Bay. and the road.

Presque Isle State Park Bikepath	
Location	Presque Isle State Park, Erie County
Trailheads	Parking lots at intervals along the trail
Length, Surface	5.8 miles; asphalt
Character	Crowded, state park, mostly shady, flat
Usage restrictions	No motorized vehicles; no horses
Amenities	Water, rest rooms, bike rental, food, swimming, fishing
Driving time from Pittsburgh	2 hours 45 minutes north

Local history, attractions

Presque Isle is a geologically unique sand spit of glacial sand. The ponds support a variety of aquatic biological successions. The location is a favorite of migratory birds, with late May and late September the prime seasons. As you move inland you go from sand beaches and wetlands to climax forest within a couple of miles.

This was a strategic location in the War of 1812. Commodore Oliver Hazard Perry's fleet was constructed here between February and June 1813. On September 10, 1813 the US fleet of nine boats engaged six British warships under Captain Robert Barclay in the Battle of Lake Erie. Flying his battle flag, "Don't Give Up the Ship", Perry defeated Barclay and returned to Misery Bay, near the Perry Monument. At the end of the battle he sent his classic message of victory, "We have met the enemy and they are ours." The Flagship Niagara historic site is nearby in Erie.

Extensions of the ride

The Peninsula Drive bike lanes, about 1 mile rolling, lead from the park entrance toward Erie on the shoulder of PA832.

It's tempting to consider continuing along the road from Perry's Monument around the end and north side of the peninsula, but the road is busy and very narrow.

Access points

Vicinity: Follow I79 north to its end in Erie. Go west on PA5 to PA832, then north (right) on PA832 to the park entrance.

Trailheads: Park in lots near the entrance or at any of a variety of other lots along the south side of the peninsula.

Amenities

Rest rooms, water: Comfort stations are located at 9 places along or near the trail.

Bike shop, rentals: Bike rentals are available along PA832 north of PA5, connected by bike lanes to the park.

Restaurant, groceries: Food and refreshment concessions are located along the trail at Beaches 6 and 8.

Camping, simple lodging: Nothing close, but motels and camping are available in and near Erie.

Swimming, fishing: At official beaches, only when lifeguard is on duty. The guarded beaches are open 10 AM to 8 PM from Memorial Day to Labor Day unless posted otherwise. Good fishing. Common catches are perch, coho, smelt, walleye, rainbow trout and bass in Lake Erie, and panfish, perch, bass, muskellunge, walleye, northern pike, crappies, smelt, and coho in Presque Isle Bay.

Winter sports: Cross-country skiing. Ice fishing.

Trail organization

Presque Isle State Park
PA Department of Environmental Resources
PO Box 8510
Erie, PA 16505
(814) 871-4251

Maps, guides, other references

USGS Topographic Maps: Swanville, Erie North

Presque Isle State Park brochure

The Western Pennsylvania Conservancy has a detailed 2-page description of walking trails on the peninsula.

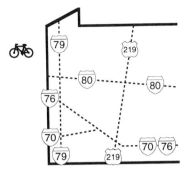

Ohio and Erie Canal Towpath Trail

Along Cuyahoga River in Cuyahoga Valley National Recreation Area

The Cuyahoga River valley has served as a transportation corridor for centuries. At some places along this trail you'll see canal and railroad beside you and modern superhighway overhead. The trail follows the towpath of the Ohio and Erie Canal, which was built between 1825 and 1832 to connect Cleveland, on Lake Erie, with the Ohio River 308 miles away. The route was from Cleveland upstream along the Cuyahoga River to Akron, then down the Tuscarawas River. Until the middle of the 19th century the canal was an economic success. However, like many canals, railroads and floods spelled its end. The final blow for this canal was the flood of 1913. Parts of the canal and traces of its heritage are now being restored in the corridor from Cleveland to Zoar. The modern-day Towpath trail runs 19.5 miles from Lock 39 in Valley View south to the northern edge of Akron. Mileage markers along the trail are based on historical mileages measured from Lake Erie, so the northern end of the trail is near milepost 11 and the southern end half a mile past milepost 30. The mileposts are not exactly a mile apart on the modern trail, so our intermediate measurements are approximate.

This trail follows the canal towpath from mile 10.75 to mile 30.3, including lock 39 to lock 24. Most of the trail surface is packed crushed stone. In some sections there is a parallel equestrian trail. Where the equestrian trail shares the towpath trail, it is hard surfaced. Other areas can get a little soft when they're wet. Confusingly, the miles are numbered starting from Cleveland, but the locks are numbered starting from Akron (both northbound and southbound). This stretch lies in the Cuyahoga Valley National Recreation Area, an "urban park". As a result, the setting is varied, but never industrial or commercial.

Ohio and Erie Canal Towpath Trail	
Location	Along Cuyahoga River in Cuyahoga Valley National Recreation Area, Cuyahoga and Summit Counties OH
Trailheads	Rockside Rd, Canal Visitor Center, Station Rd Bridge, Redlock, Boston, Peninsula, Hunt Farm, Ira, Indian Mound (Bath Rd)
Length, Surface	19.5 miles, mostly crushed stone with some hardtop where equestrian trail overlaps
Character	busy; suburban to rural, wooded; shady; flat
Usage restrictions	Horse trail partly overlaps towpath trail; no motorized vehicles; no snowmobiles
Amenities	Rest rooms, water, bike rental, food, lodging, swimming, fishing
Driving time from Pittsburgh	2 hours 30 minutes northwest

The trail currently starts at a trailhead parking lot (mile 10.75). The canal holds water for the next six miles or so, nearly to Station Road Bridge. For the first three and a half miles the canal is squeezed between the river and the road. The road is not intrusive, though, as the towpath is on the river side of the canal. The Canal Visitor Center is in a restored canal-era two-story frame building next to the restored lock at mile 12.5; you can view interpretive exhibits or pick up maps or other information here. To the west, bottomlands separate you from the river; to the east, across the road from the visitor center, is a historic house. Just past mile 13 the trail and canal cross Tinker's Creek on an aqueduct, one of 14 on the entire canal.

At mile 14 the trail passes another lock, this one beside a grist mill. Alexander's Mill, now called Wilson's Mill, was built in 1855 to use water bypassing the lock to power its grinding wheel. It had an interior horizontal turbine rather than the more common overshot wheel. It continued to use water power until 1972, when it was converted to electrical power. Just south of the grist mill, a waste weir provides control over the water level in the canal, both to maintain the working water level and to prevent flooding. The mechanical apparatus is visible and functional; it's not hard to understand how the gates were raised and lowered. In another quarter-mile, the Frazee House appears across the canal. This Federal style house was restored by the National Park Service and serves as a museum of life in the Western Reserve.

Grist mill alongside canal, mile 14

Just past the Frazee house, the road swings away and the canal, the river, and the railroad all squeeze through a narrow gorge called Pinery Narrows that runs to the OH82 bridge. The 2.5-mile section from mile 14.4 to 16.9 is the most isolated and tranquil section of the trail. You're likely to see ducks, geese, deer, and other wildlife here. The end of the Narrows is marked overhead by OH82 and underfoot by the remains of Lock 36 and the feeder dam and canal that supplied water to the lower end of the canal. This is the end of the watered section of the canal. From here south, your imagination will have to put the canal back in its prism.

Just past OH82 (mile 17.1), the historic Station Road Bridge has been restored to connect the trail with the Brecksville Reservation of the Cleveland Metroparks and parking. The bridge is paved in wooden blocks, end-grain up. At mile 18.3 and 18.8, footbridges provide access to the Old Carriage Trail, which meanders for 3.25 miles on the other side of the canal. It also provides a connecting link to the Bike & Hike trail on the plateau at the top of the valley. Bicycles are permitted only on the direct path from the mile 18.8 bridge to the Bike & Hike trail.

The valley around the canal gradually becomes more developed as you go south. Across the river on Highland Rd, for example, is the former Jaite Paper Mill company town. These buildings are now used as National Park Service Headquarters. On the towpath just south of Highland Rd (mile 19.6) you'll see the remains of a corrugated box company; this was the Jaite Mill. A side trail a mile 20.95 takes you to Stanford Farm Youth Hostel and onward to Brandywine Falls. At mile 21.5 the trail reach Boston Mills Rd. While the building alongside the trail is being renovated (in 1996), jog left a quarter mile to pick up the towpath again at the trailhead parking lot. Between here and mile 22 the trail passes under I271 and I80 far overhead.

From mile 22.3 to mile 22.6, a boardwalk carries the trail over Stumpy basin. This was originally a turning basin and work area on the canal. The river has reclaimed part of the towpath and turned the basin into a swamp. In any case, this is now a good area for viewing wildlife. At mile 23, the towpath clings to the side of the cliff; here too the river has reclaimed part of the canal. The remains of another feeder canal appear near Lock 30 (mile 23.4). At mile 23.7 you can cross over to the Peninsula parking area or continue on the towpath, crossing the Cuyahoga river on an aqueduct. If you leave the towpath here you can visit the town of Peninsula, the chief source of food or other services in the area. The town, once larger then Cleveland, began as a canal town during the canal's heyday in the mid-19th century. Now it is on the National Register of Historic Places.

Continuing south from Peninsula, the towpath passes Deep Lock quarry, reachable by a side trail, and Deep Lock. Deep Lock is so-called because it has a 17′ lift instead of the usual 9′. The Berea Sandstone quarry nearby provided stone for canal structures and was a major source of millstones for the region. The valley here is predominantly rural, with farms and villages dotting the valley. Another visitor center at mile 27 offers information and amenities. At mile 28 the beaver have won out over the canal, and another boardwalk carries the trail over swamp for a tenth of a mile. The Beaver Marsh area was once an auto junkyard; when the cars were removed, it reverted to a natural marsh. From Ira (mile 28.5) the road was constructed between the canal and the river, so close to the canal that parts of the towpath and even of locks 24 and 25 were replaced by roadway. Here the trail is on the west side of the road, not always on the original towpath. Mile 30.5 is the Indian Mound trailhead and the current end of the trail.

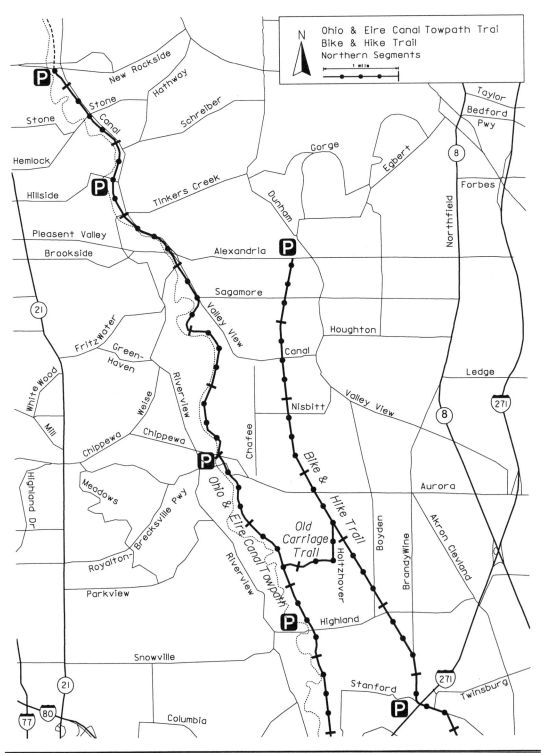

Ohio & Eire Canal Towpath Trail
Bike & Hike Trail
Northern Segments

1 mile

New Rockside
Hathway
Stone
Canal
Schreiber
Stone
Hemlock
Hillside
Pleasent Valley
Brookside
Tinkers Creek
Gorge
Egbert
Dunham
Alexandria
Sagamore
21
Valley View
FritzWater
Green-Haven
Houghton
Canal
Whitewood
Riverview
Weise
Nisbitt
Ledge
Mill
Chafee
Chippewa
Chippewa
Meadows
Brecksville Pwy
Highland Dr
Royalton-
Ohio & Eire Canal Towpath
Old Carriage Trail
Bike & Hike Trail
Aurora
Boyden
BrandyWine
Akron Cleveland
Parkview
Riverview
Holtzhover
Snowville
Highland
Columbia
Stanford
Twinsburg
271
21
77
80

Taylor
Bedford Pwy
8
Forbes
Northfield
8
271

Extensions of the ride

The historic Cuyahoga Valley Scenic Railroad parallels the towpath for the entire length of the trail. Most of the trailheads are also boarding areas for the scenic railroad. It is possible to arrange bike/train options; call (800) 468-4070 for current information.

The Old Carriage Trail offers a 3.25-mile excursion for walkers only.

Part of the Old Carriage Trail can be used to connect with the Bike & Hike Trail on the rim of the valley At the mile 18.8 bridge that links the towpath to the Old Carriage Road, bikes can start up the hill. The trail emerges at the end of Holzhauer Rd; go north for half a mile to the intersection with the Bike & Hike trail. By following the Bike & Hike trail north, you can also connect with the Bedford Reservation all-purpose trail of Cleveland Metroparks.

At the Station Road Bridge trailhead you're not far from the Brecksville Reservation all-purpose trail of Cleveland Metroparks. Go out Station Rd to Riverview Rd and pick up the all-purpose trail at the end of Chippewa Creek Parkway.

At Deep Lock you can explore the quarry on walking trails (not suitable for bicycles).

Information centers can supply maps for bicycle tours on park roads.

Development plans

Plans call for extending the towpath northward by 6 miles and southward by 2 miles. These sections were not yet accessible at the beginning of 1996.

Access points

Vicinity: Directions begin on Riverview Rd, at Boston Mills Rd. Riverview Rd runs along the Cuyahoga River for much of the length of the National Recreation area. To reach this point from Pittsburgh, go west on the PA Turnpike to the state line and continue 60 miles on the Ohio Turnpike. Leave the Ohio Turnpike at Exit 12 (Akron, OH8) headed south on OH8. At the first traffic light, turn right (west) on Boston Mills Rd and go about 5 miles to Riverview Rd, just after you cross the river.

Lock 39 (northern) trailhead and Canal Visitor Center: At the intersection of Boston Mills Rd and Riverview Rd, turn right (north) on Riverview Rd and go about 8-9 miles to the intersection with Brookside Rd. Turn right on Brookside and go a short distance to Pleasant Valley Rd. Go east on Pleasant Valley Rd to the Canal Rd exit and then go north. For the Canal Visitor Center, go north about 1.5 miles to Hillside Rd; turn left and cross the canal to the parking lot. For the Lock 39 trailhead, go north about 3 miles to Rockside Rd; turn left and cross the canal. The parking lot will be on the left.

Station Road Bridge trailhead: At the intersection of Boston Mills Rd and Riverview Rd, turn right (north) on Riverview Rd and go about 5 miles to the Station Road Bridge parking area.

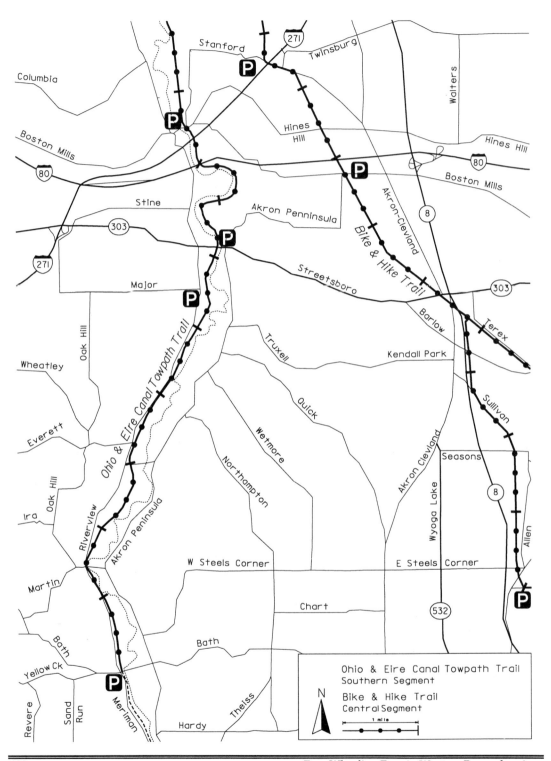

Columbia

Stanford

271

Twinsburg

Walters

Boston Mills

80

Hines
Hill

Hines Hill

80

Stine

Akron Penninsula

Boston Mills

8

303

271

Major

Streetsboro

Akron-Clevland

Bike & Hike Trail

303

Oak Hill

Wheatley

Truxell

Barlow

Kendall Park

Terex

Everett

Quick

Sullivan

Oak Hill

Ohio & Eire Canal Towpath Trail

Wetmore

Akron Cleviand

Seasons

Ira

Northampton

Wyoga Lake

8

Riverview

Akron Peninsula

Allen

Martin

W Steels Corner

E Steels Corner

Bath

Chart

532

Bath

Yellow Ck

Meriman

Theiss

Revere

Sand Run

Hardy

Ohio & Eire Canal Towpath Trail
Southern Segment

N

Bike & Hike Trail
Central Segment

1 mile

Boston trailhead: Instead of following Boston Mills Rd all the way to Riverview Rd, turn left into the trailhead parking lot just after the road reaches valley level, about a quarter-mile before crossing the river.

Lock 29 (Peninsula) trailhead: At the intersection of Boston Mills Rd and Riverview Rd, turn left (south) on Riverview Rd and go about 1.5 miles to OH303 (Streetsboro Rd). Turn left (east) on OH303, cross the Cuyahoga River, and turn left at the traffic light 1 block east of the river. Follow signs to the trailhead.

Hunt Farm visitor center, Ira and Indian Mound (southern) trailheads: At the intersection of Boston Mills Rd and Riverview Rd, turn left (south) on Riverview Rd and go about 5 miles to the Hunt Farm visitor center, 7 miles to the Ira trailhead, or 9 miles to the Indian Mound trailhead.

Amenities

Rest rooms, water: At Canal Visitor Center, Station Road Bridge trailhead, Lock 29 (Peninsula) trailhead, Hunt Farm information center, Indian Mound trailhead.

Bike shop, rental: In Peninsula.

Restaurant, groceries: In Peninsula.

Camping, simple lodging: AYH Stanford Farm Hostel 1.5 miles down a steep rough road from Brandywine Falls or 0.5 miles from Boston on Stanford Rd. The Inn at Brandywine Falls. Dover Lake campground on Highland Rd near the Cuyahoga River.

Swimming, fishing: Swimming and other water activities at Dover Lake Waterpark (fee). Fishing in Cuyahoga River subject to Ohio fishing regulations.

Winter sports: Cross-country skiing.

Trail organization

Cuyahoga Valley National Recreation Area
15610 Vaughn Rd
Brecksville OH 44141
(216) 524-1497

Maps, guides, other references

The Ohio & Erie Canal Towpath Trail, trail brochure.

Cuyahoga Valley National Recreation Area, National Park Service brochure.

Ohio & Erie Canal Corridor Guide, Ohio & Erie Canal Corridor Coalition, PO Box 435, Canal Fulton, OH 44614

Trail Guide Handbook, Cuyahoga Valley Trails Council, 1991.

USGS Topographic Maps: Cleveland South, Shaker Heights, Northfield, Peninsula

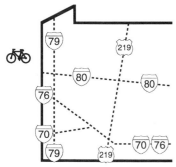

Bike and Hike Trail (to Kent and Stow OH)

From Walton Hills to Kent and Stow, Ohio

The Bike and Hike Trail follows the routes of a former railroad, the New York Central, and two former interurban trolley lines, the Akron, Bedford, and Cleveland (or "alphabet" railroad) and another branch of the Northern Ohio Traction & Light Company. It features a variety of terrain along the route. The trail runs roughly as a "Y" with the base of the stem near Cleveland and arms reaching to Kent and Stow. The junction, where the arms join the stem, is just east of OH8. Most of the road crossings are at grade level, so watch for traffic.

The northern end of the trail is at Alexander Rd, just west of Dunham Rd, where a parking area serves both the Bike & Hike Trail and the Cleveland Metroparks Bedford all-purpose trail (see Emerald Necklace trail description). The Bike & Hike trail runs south on a crushed limestone surface along the former route of the New York Central Railroad. In half a mile, at Sagamore Rd, a high-voltage electric transmission line joins the trail. For the next 2.5 miles the electric line and the trail coexist, exposed to the summer sun. This segment is somewhat less scenic than the rest of the trail.

At the Highland Rd crossing, responsibility for the trail shifts from Cleveland to Summit county. Mileage signs along the southern part of the trail appear to count from here. At Brandywine Rd, about 5 miles from Alexander Rd, the trail emerges on Brandywine Road, joining Brandywine Road for a mile to cross over I271. Just north of the I271 bridge, it passes Brandywine Falls. This area of the Cuyahoga National Recreation area features a 75-foot waterfall and old mill. A boardwalk descends from the parking area to the falls, one of the highest in Ohio. A B&B overlooks the falls from the opposite side. Half a mile past I271, the trail returns to the railroad grade and runs through open woods for 1.5 miles to Boston Mills Road. After you pass Boston Mills road you'll be reminded that Ohio isn't flat, for the railroad grade runs past fine rock formations in cuts and on fill for most of a mile; this area is called Boston Ledges. After emerging from the cuts and fills, the trail becomes suburban again, cross under OH303 and over OH8, and arrives at a "Y" junction. Here the trail splits, running separately to Stow and Kent. The north branch, to Stow, runs on the railbed of the Akron, Bedford, and Cleveland, a former interurban trolley line. Early this century, the AB&C merged with other Akron services to form the Northern Ohio Traction & Light Company; service ended in 1932.

At the "Y" junction you can go left for 5.2 miles to Silver Spring Park and Stow or right for 11.4 miles to Munroe Falls and Kent. The sign also says you've come 5.3 miles south from Sagamore Hills and Highland Road, ignoring the 5 miles to the north of Highland Road (you're actually 10 miles from the trailhead at Alexander Road).

If you go left from the "Y" junction toward Stow, the character of the trail remains much the same -- open woods, glimpses of suburbia, and occasional road crossings at grade.

4.5 miles from the junction the trail passes the swimming lake at Silver Spring Park, where (for a fee) you can take a dip in the summer. The trail ends at Young Rd 5.2 miles from the junction. At this point you can go right (south) half a mile on the road and pick up the Stow bikeway to the high school on Graham Rd in Stow.

Bike and Hike Trail	
Location	Walton Hills to Kent and Stow, Cuyahoga and Summit Counties OH
Trailheads	Walton Hills, Brandywine Falls, Boston Mills, Silver Springs Park, Springdale, Munroe Falls
Length, Surface	29 miles, asphalt and crushed stone (1 mile on-street near Brandywine Falls; 3.3 miles on-street in Stow and Silver Lake
Character	busy, suburban; sunny; flat in north, hilly in south, with short steep hills at many road crossings
Usage restrictions	No motorized vehicles, no snowmobiles, no horses
Amenities	Rest rooms, water, food, swimming, fishing
Driving time from Pittsburgh	2 hours 20 minutes northwest

If you go right from the junction toward Kent, you'll find a very different kind of riding ahead. At first the trail continues through open woods and rural residences. 2.5 miles past the junction, though, it emerges alongside OH8. The surface changes to asphalt here, but the trail becomes hilly and noisy. After a mile of highway, the trail takes a quick dip for a tenth of a mile through the woods, then emerges at the intersection of busy Hudson Rd and Springdale Rd. There's trailhead parking just ahead on Springdale Rd. The next 3.3 miles are on roads. The intersections are well-marked, but there are a few long stretches where it would be nice to have some reassurance that you're still on track. After half a mile on Springdale Rd, the trail turns right into a residential area of Stow reminiscent of an Audubon Society meeting: it rolls up and down Goldfinch, Whippoorwill, Meadowlark, and Hummingbird. Eventually it crosses Graham Rd and enters the upscale community of Silver Lake, still with rolling hills. At Kent, the trail ducks down a dirt road and enters a park to become a motor-free trail again. Now it follows the Cuyahoga River, winding and still somewhat hilly. This is one of the best sections for wildlife, especially large birds along the river. The Kelsey Bike Trail branches off in this area (it goes south across the river to Waterworks and Galt Parks). After 4.5 miles along the river, the trail finally ends on North River Rd 11.4 miles from the junction near OH8.

Many of the road crossings must once have been underpasses -- at many crossings you must ride up a brisk (though short) hill to the road, then cross and ride right back down again. The former bridges have been converted to fill, and the cost of converting all these crossings back to bridges would be prohibitive. To further complicate matters, many of the trail gates at the road crossings have very narrow openings, sometimes with sharp drops from the pavement. Be careful at these gates; you may want to walk your bike.

Extensions of the ride

The northern end of the Bike & Hike Trail connects with the Bedford Reservation segment of the Cleveland Metroparks all-purpose trail. See the Emerald Necklace trail description for details about where this takes you.

You can also connect with the Ohio & Erie Canal towpath via the Old Carriage Trail. When the Bike & Hike Trail crosses Holzhauer Rd (the first road south of OH82), turn south on Holzhauer Rd and follow it half a mile to its end. Bear right on another crushed stone path, which descends steeply to the towpath along part of the Old Carriage Trail. You'll emerge on the towpath just north of milepost 19. Remember that you'll have to get back up somehow. See the Ohio & Erie Canal trail description for details about how this connects to the towpath.

Brandywine Falls

At the end of the Stow branch, you can turn right (south) on Young Rd, go about half a mile on this lightly-traveled road, and turn right (west) onto the Stow Bikeway. This currently runs almost 2 miles to the Stow/Munroe Falls High School on Graham Rd in

Stow. Someday it will be extended to connect with the southern branch of the Bike & Hike Trail near Kent, completing the loop.

On the Kent/Munroe Falls branch, shortly after the trail joins the Cuyahoga River at Kent Park, the Kelsey Bikeway branches off to the south. Operated by the City of Cuyahoga Falls, it goes about a mile south across the Cuyahoga River, connecting to Waterworks Park and Galt Park

On the map, this trail looks like a curving "Y", with the open end to the east of southeast. Your immediate reaction is probably that you'd like to close the open end to form a loop -- that was certainly ours. The Stow Bike Trail takes you more than half-way across, but it leaves you on busy Graham Rd. Plans call for extending Stow Bike Trail to close the loop. Until then, here's the best route we've found: When the Kent branch of the trail ends at North River Rd, turn right on North River Rd for one block. Turn left on Meadow, go one block, and turn left on Francis St. Follow Francis St for four blocks to Main St and turn left on Main St at the traffic light. There are restaurants here, virtually the only ones we found along the trail. If you're hungry, you can eat Geppetto's barbecued ribs in the shadow of his rib cook-off trophies. After eating or not, as the case may be, go one block west from Francis St on Main St and turn right on Spaulding Dr. Go one block on Spaulding Dr, then turn left on Silver Meadows Blvd and follow it a half-mile or so through a series of apartment buildings until it ends at Fairfield Av. Turn left on Fairfield Av, then take the next right on Newcomer Rd. Go about 1 mile on Newcomer Rd and take the first left, on Young Rd. After about half a mile on Young Rd, you'll pass a trailhead for the Stow bikeway. We don't know where it goes, but it isn't the trail you're looking for. Your turn onto the Bike and Hike Trail is almost half a mile later, not far after you cross Call Rd. Total distance on roads is just under 4 miles.

Access points

Vicinity: Directions begin at Exit 12 (Akron, OH8) of the Ohio Turnpike. To reach this point from Pittsburgh, go west on the PA Turnpike to the state line and continue 60 miles on the Ohio Turnpike.

North (Alexander Rd) trailhead: From Exit 12 of the Ohio Turnpike, go north about 7.5 miles on OH8 to Alexander Rd. Turn left on Alexander Rd and go about 2 miles to trailhead parking, just past Dunham Rd.

Brandywine Falls trailhead: From Exit 12 of the Ohio Turnpike, go north to the first traffic light, Hines Rd. Turn left on Hines Rd and go about half a mile to Cleveland Rd. Turn right, then immediately take the left fork, Brandywine Rd. Follow Brandywine Rd a little over a mile until it crosses over I271. (At this point the trail will be sharing the shoulder of the road.) Just as you come off the bridge, turn left into the Brandywine Falls parking area.

Boston Mills trailhead: From Exit 12 of the Ohio Turnpike, go south on OH8 to the first traffic light. At this light, turn right (west) on Boston Mills Rd and go 1 mile to trailhead parking.

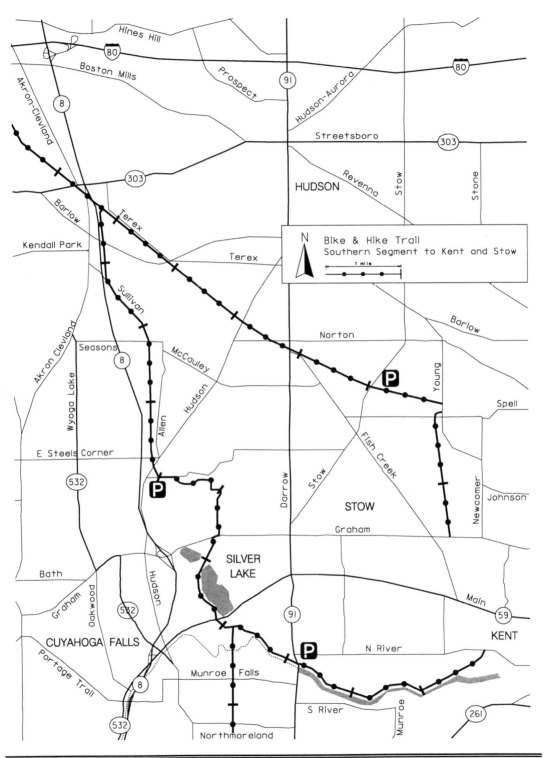

Bike & Hike Trail
Southern Segment to Kent and Stow

1 mile

Silver Springs Park trailhead: From Exit 12 of the Ohio Turnpike, go south on OH8 just over 2 miles to Barlow Rd. Turn left (east) on Barlow Rd. Follow Barlow Rd about 4 miles to Stow Rd. Turn right (south) on Stow Rd, then turn left to park at Silver Springs Park.

Springdale Rd trailhead: From Exit 12 of the Ohio Turnpike, go south on OH8 just over 2 miles to Barlow Rd. Turn left (east) on Barlow Rd. Follow Barlow Rd just over 2 miles to Darrow Rd. Turn right (south) on Darrow Rd make the first right turn, on Hudson Dr. Go about 3.5 miles on Hudson Dr to Springdale Rd (the trail crosses here). Turn left (east) on Springdale Rd and go half a block to trailhead parking.

Munroe Falls (Darrow Rd) trailhead: From Exit 12 of the Ohio Turnpike, go south on OH8 just over 2 miles to Barlow Rd. Turn left (east) on Barlow Rd. Follow Barlow Rd just over 2 miles to Darrow Rd. Turn right (south) on Darrow Rd and go just over 5 miles to trailhead parking, just before you cross the Cuyahoga River.

Amenities

Rest rooms, water: Rest rooms at Brandywine Falls area of Cuyahoga Valley National Recreation Area, the Darrow Rd trailhead in Munroe Falls, and (in season) the Silver Springs swimming area near the end of the Stow branch. Portable toilets at the Silver Lake recreation area where the trail leaves the road near Kent Rd and at Silver Springs park. Water at Silver Springs park. The Wagon Wheel lounge 0.1 mile north of the trail junction will fill your water bottle for $.50.

Bike shop, rental: In town of Peninsula in Cuyahoga National Recreation Area.

Restaurant, groceries: Wagon Wheel lounge 0.1 mile north of the trail junction. Several restaurants near the intersection of Francis Rd and Main St 0.7 mile from the end of the Kent branch, along the extension on roads that connects Kent to Stow.

Camping, simple lodging: AYH Stanford Farm Hostel 1.5 miles down a steep rough road from Brandywine Falls or 0.5 miles from Boston on Stanford Rd. The Inn at Brandywine Falls. Budget Inn 0.1 mile north of trail junction near OH8.

Swimming, fishing: Swimming at swim lake, Silver Springs Park (fee); there's an entry from the trail. Swimming at Munroe Falls Metro Park (fee in season); from Munroe Falls parking lot on Darrow Rd, go south 1 mile on Darrow Rd and left (east) 1 more mile on South River Rd to park entrance. Fishing in Cuyahoga River at various points along last 4 miles of Kent Branch. Favorite fishing spots are the section of the trail between Silver Lake Village and Darrow Rd and the area just upstream from the dam and trailhead parking in Munroe Falls. Primary catches are large- and smallmouth bass, northern pike, and channel catfish. The extremely attractive park alongside the trail as it runs through Silver Lake Estates is private.

Winter sports: Cross-country skiing. Naturalists from Metro Parks, Serving Summit County offer organized ski excursions. Snowmobiling is not permitted.

Trail organization

Metro Parks, Serving Summit County Section

Thomas Shuster, Director
Metro Parks, Serving Summit County
975 Treaty Line Road
Akron OH 44313-5898

(330) 867-5511

Cleveland Metroparks Section

Steven Coles, Chief of Park Planning
Cleveland Metroparks
4101 Fulton Parkway
Cleveland OH 44144-1923

(216) 351-6300

Maps, guides, other references

Trail brochure from Metro Parks, Serving Summit County

Trail Guide Handbook, Cuyahoga Valley Trails Council, 1991.

USGS Topographic Maps: Northfield, Peninsula, Hudson,

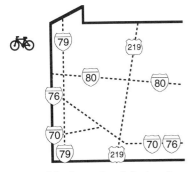

Emerald Necklace

Cleveland Metroparks surrounding Cleveland OH

The Cleveland Metroparks system includes 19,000 acres of public land including 100 miles of parkways and 12 "reservations" for recreational activities. The system is called the "Emerald Necklace" because the lands nearly encircle the city of Cleveland. Ten of the reservations include paved all-purpose trails for cycling, walking, jogging, in-line skating, and other activities. The surface is suitable for wheelchairs, but some of the trails are hilly and some grades are steep.

Six of the all-purpose trails can be combined with each other and with three nearby trails (Bike & Hike Trail, Old Carriage Trail, and Ohio & Erie Canal Towpath) for long rides. Two gaps, of 2 and 9 miles, prevent this from being a fully-connected system. However, those gaps are covered by Metroparks parkway roads, which are not too bad for cycling -- and the 2-mile gap is scheduled to get a trail.

All of the trails are park trails, running past picnic areas and recreational areas such as ballfields. They also visit nature centers, geologic features, and historic sites. Trail access is not an issue, as the trails are near, often in sight of, roads and parking is abundant near picnic areas.

The portion of the necklace to the east of the 9-mile gap includes 18.3 miles of all-purpose trail, 6.6 miles of connections on other trails, and 2 miles of road.

South Chagrin Reservation all-purpose trail	8.5 miles
West end meets Bedford-Chagrin Parkway	
Bedford-Chagrin Parkway (road)	2.0 miles
East end meets South Chagrin Reservation	
West end meets Bedford Reservation	
Bedford Reservation all-purpose trail	5.3 miles
East end meets Bedford-Chagrin Parkway	
South end meets Bike & Hike trail	
Bike & Hike Trail to Holzhauer Rd	4.0 miles
North end meets Bedford Reservation	
Old Carriage Trail connector on Holzhauer Rd	
Old Carriage Trail	0.6 miles
East end meets Bike & Hike Trail at Holzhauer Rd	
West end meets Ohio & Erie Towpath at mile 18.8	
Ohio & Erie Canal from Old Carriage Trail to Station Rd Bridge	2.0 miles
Meets Old Carriage Trail at mile 18.8	
Meets Brecksville Reservation across river from mile 17.1	
Brecksville Reservation all-purpose trail	4.5 miles
East end meets Ohio&Erie Canal	

The west end of the southern branch of the Brecksville reservation trail puts you on a road, the Royalton-Brecksville Parkway. This leads, in about 9 miles, to the east end of the Mill Stream Run reservation.

The portion of the necklace to the west of the 9-mile gap includes 29 miles of all-purpose trail:

Mill Stream Run Reservation all-purpose trail	4.0 miles
West end meets Rocky River Reservation (South)	
Big Creek Reservation all-purpose trail	7.5 miles
South end meets Rocky River Reservation (South)	
Rocky River Reservation (South) all-purpose trail	7.0 miles
East end meets Mill Stream Run Reservation	
Branch near east end meets Big Creek Reservation	
North end meets Rocky River Reservation (North)	
Rocky River Reservation (North) all-purpose trail	10.5 miles
South end meets Rocky River Reservation (South)	

Emerald Necklace	
Location	An arc around Cleveland, in Cuyahoga County OH
Trailheads	Many picnic areas in the Cleveland Metroparks system
Length, Surface	47 miles of all-purpose trails, 8' asphalt
Character	crowded; urban; shady; hilly
Usage restrictions	No horses, no motor vehicles
Amenities	Rest rooms, water, food, swimming, fishing
Driving time from Pittsburgh (to Bedford)	2 hours 40 minutes northwest

Access points

Any good city map of Cleveland will show the locations of the Metroparks reservations. There is no shortage of access to the trails. To get you started, we provide access points to the eastern and western segments.

Vicinity: Directions begin headed west on the Ohio Turnpike approaching Exit 12. To reach this point from Pittsburgh, go west on the PA Turnpike to the state line and continue 60 miles on the Ohio Turnpike.

Bedford Reservation / Alexander Rd trailhead: Take Exit 12 of the Ohio Turnpike headed north on OH8. Go north about 7.5 miles on OH8 to Alexander Rd. Turn left on Alexander Rd and go about 2 miles to trailhead parking, just past Dunham Rd.

Mill Stream Run and Rock River (South) Pearl Rd trailhead: Take Exit 10 of the Ohio Turnpike headed south on US42. Go south on US22 about half a mile to Albion Rd. Turn left on Albion Rd and stop at the first convenient picnic area.

Amenities

Rest rooms, water: At many picnic areas throughout the reservations.

Bike shop, rental: Many in and around Cleveland.

Restaurant, groceries: Refreshment stands in the park. Many other stores near the park.

Camping, simple lodging: Nearby in numerous places.

Swimming, fishing: Swimming at Wallace/Baldwin Lake area in Rocky River Reservation (South). Fishing at Shadow Lake in South Chagrin Reservation, Ranger Lake and Bonnie Park picnic area in Mill Stream Run Reservation, the entire length of Rocky River, Wallace/Baldwin Lake area and Lagoon picnic area in Rocky River Reservation (South), Scenic Park marina and Rockcliff Springs in Rocky River Reservation (North).

Winter sports: Cross-country skiing.

Trail organization

Cleveland Metroparks System
4101 Fulton Parkway
Cleveland OH 44144-1923
(216) 351-6300

Maps, guides, other references

A Guide to the Cleveland Metroparks System. Folded map, Cleveland Metroparks System.

Trail Guide Handbook, Cuyahoga Valley Trails Council, 1991.

USGS Topographic Maps: Chagrin Falls, Shaker Heights, Northfield, Broadview Heights, Berea, Lakewood, North Olmstead, Cleveland South

Rails-to-Trails Conservancy

Most of the trails described here started life as railroads. As the US rail system has shrunk, many of the abandoned rights-of-way are gaining new life as recreational trails. A national nonprofit organization, the Rails-to-Trails Conservancy, coordinates these conversion efforts. The 10-year-old RTC has over 62,000 members nationally, 7,000 in Pennsylvania. Support for trail development includes

⇒ Notifying trail advocates and local governments of upcoming abandonments
⇒ Assisting public and private groups with legal details about trail acquisition
⇒ Providing technical help to private citizens and trail developers
⇒ Publicizing rail-to-trail issues throughout the country

In Pennsylvania, over 75 rail-trails are open, under active development, or in some stage of planning. 19 of those are represented in this guide. To add your support to this organization, contact either the state chapter or the national office. They do take Mastercard and Visa.

Pa Chapter, Rails-to-Trails Conservancy
105 Locust St
Harrisburg PA 17101
(717) 238-1717

Rails-to-Trails Conservancy
1400 16th St NW, Suite 300
Washington DC 20036
(202) 797-5400

Annual membership: $18 individual, $25 family, $50 organization, $100 benefactor

About This Guidebook

We created this guidebook to support development of the trail systems. First, by making more people aware of the trails, we help to build the community of users. Second, we will contribute part of the proceeds from sales to trail development, and we will provide discounted copies of the book to trail councils for their use in fund-raising.

For additional copies of this guidebook, check with your favorite trail council, local bicycle shop, outfitter, or bookstore. If they don't have any, ask them to order some. If you'd rather order directly from us, send a check for $11.97 per copy (that's $9.95 + $.70 tax + $1.32 shipping and handling) with your name and address to

Shaw-Weil Associates
414 South Craig St, #307
Pittsburgh PA 15213

Ask for *FreeWheeling Easy in Western Pennsylvania*. Sorry—no cash, credit cards, or COD. You can also let us know if you want to be notified when the next edition is published.

August 1997 Supplement

Since publication of this edition in spring of 1996, a number of new trail segments have opened. This supplement describes several new trail segments that have been completed in the past year and a half:

Montour Trail, Quicksilver to McDonald
Montour Trail, South Park Section
Shorter Trails near Pittsburgh:
      Lawrenceville Trail
      Downtown to Oakland Riverview Trail
Five Star Trail

We also add the excellent trail system in the northern panhandle of West Virginia:

    Wheeling Heritage Trails

There have been some noteworthy changes to the trails of the second edition:

Three Rivers Heritage Trail (p.11): Plans are moving ahead to refurbish the railroad bridge that connects the downstream tip of Washington Landing to the trail near its current end along River Rd. On the North Side, several construction projects have created trail detours. The trail will be restored when construction is completed.

Montour Trail, Robinson-Moon-Findlay-North Fayette Section (p.17): There's now a bike shop beside the trail at Imperial.

Montour Trail, Cecil Township Section (p.22): The trail council is working toward installing a bridge at Hendersonville in 1998.

Youghiogheny River Trail, Northern Section (p. 36): The trail is now open from Adelaide to Connellsville, connecting there to the Southern Section. Stone Bridge Trail, a spur trail up the hill (it's a big hill!) from Dawson to Linden Hall has also opened. The trail map on p. 46 has been revised to show these two new sections. In addition, by October 1997 the trail should be extended a mile north from the Boston access area to the Allegheny Land Trust's Conservation Area at Dead Man's Hollow.

Chesapeake and Ohio Canal Towpath (p.61): Major floods in January and September of 1996 devastated the Towpath. It is now open again, including the hiker-biker campsites, but it's rougher in some areas than it was in the past.

Armstrong Trail (p.99): The first completed section, 1.4 miles from Tub Mill Run to 14th St in Ford City, is expected to open in late summer 1997. It will be paved, 10' wide.

We'd like to thank Larry Ridenour, Bob McKinley, Jack Paulik, Dave Carlson, and Dave Wright for their help in preparing this supplement.

Montour Trail, McDonald Section

Quicksilver to McDonald Trestle

Spring of 1997 brought the official opening of a new section of the trail in Robinson Township, Washington County. This fills in almost a third of the gap between the Imperial and Cecil Township sections. This is one of the more remote sections of the Montour Trail. It parallels PA980 through an area of former strip mines. Although the road is never far away, it is never intrusive. The trail is separated from the road by a creek and often some buildings, so you can concentrate on the surrounding scenery and nature's success in restoring the land.

This section begins just north of Beagle Club Rd on the east side of PA980 at a point with no road access. After 0.8 mile it crosses PA980, just south of the entrance to Quicksilver Golf Course, and continues another 3 miles to Noblestown Rd just west of PA980.

From Beagle Club Rd to PA980 the trail is largely on a raised embankment. The trail surface has not yet been laid, so it's pretty rough. There's no bridge at PA980, so you must scrabble down a steep hill to the road. Cross the road carefully, as sight lines for traffic are obscured. This is, for now, a dead-end stretch; access it from the PA980 end. The trail council is working toward layng trail surface in fall 1997 and installing a bridge here in 1998. This section is still for the truly dedicated.

Montour Trail, Quicksilver Section	
Location	Robinson Township, Washington County
Trailheads	Near Quicksilver, under McDonald trestle
Length, Surface	3.8 miles, crushed stone
Character	Little-used, rural, sunny, flat
Usage restrictions	No motorized vehicles; no snowmobiles
Amenities	Food
Driving time from Pittsburgh	40 minutes south-southwest

Directly across PA980, things change. A dirt driveway climbs a short steep hill to a small parking area on the west side of PA980. This is just south of the Quicksilver entrance, and it's the start of three miles of smooth trail with no road crossings. Heading south from this parking area, you pass behind a few houses, through a cut, and behind some more houses. The trail then swings away from the road, and a creek and swampy area separate the trail from the road. The houses give way to light industry, chiefly storage areas for construction equipment and materials. After a few of these, nothing obstructs the views across the valley.

As you approach the McDonald trestle (which is unfinished and closed) the trail bends left and descends to Noblestown Rd. At Noblestown Road the trail emerges near the base of the high trestle that will eventually carry the trail across this valley.

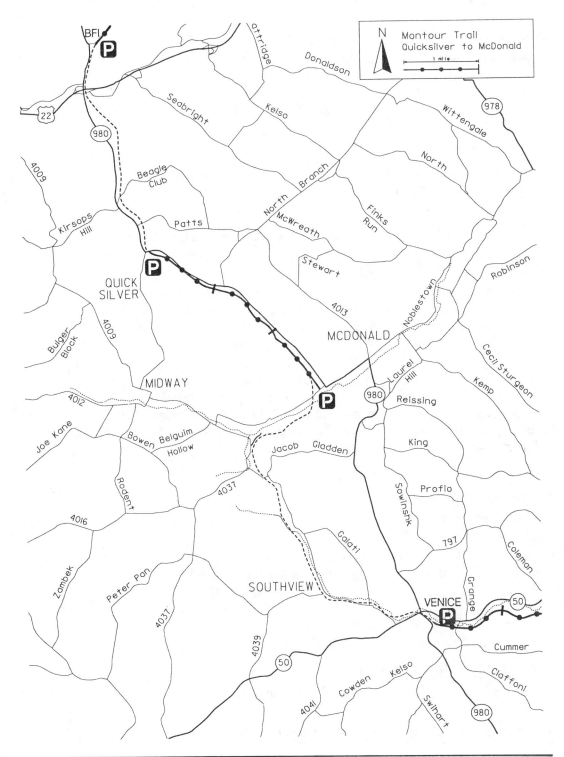

Extensions of the ride

PA980 is too busy for our tastes, but if you want to ride in traffic you can follow PA980 north from the Quicksilver crossing about 3 miles to the BFI end of the northern section of the trail. At the intersection with US22, the route number changes to SR3071. Half a mile later, turn right on SR3070 (Boggs Rd) toward the BFI landfill. Shortly after the turn, go straight into trailhead parking.

Development plans

Completion of the 2.2 miles of trail between Beagle Club Rd and the BFI trailhead to the north depends on completion of mining operations. It is not clear how long this will be.

Access points

Vicinity: Directions begin headed south from I279/US22/US30 (Parkway West) on I79 toward the Carnegie Exit (Exit 13, PA50). To reach this point from Pittsburgh, go west on I279 and turn south on I79.

South trailhead (McDonald Trestle): From I79, take the Carnegie Exit (Exit 13) and go west on Noblestown Rd for 10.6 miles. Be careful not to lose track of Noblestown Rd in Oakdale; its a little tricky. Continue through McDonald to the point where PA980 turns right on Robinson Hwy. The entrance to trailhead parking is just ahead on the left (before the trestle). The trail starts on the right, directly across from the parking lot.

North trailhead (Quicksilver): From I79, take the Carnegie Exit (Exit 13) and go west on Noblestown Rd for 10.6 miles as for the South trailhead. Turn right on PA980/Noblestown Hwy and go north for 3.0 miles. Just before the Quicksilver entrance, a sign indicates trailhead parking; a gravel driveway goes up a short hill to the parking area.

Amenities

Rest rooms, water: None

Bike shop, rentals: None directly on the trail. Closest is in Imperial, next to that section of the Montour Trail.

Restaurant, groceries: A dairy stand and a restaurant on PA980 about halfway between the trailheads. Unfortunately, they aren't accessible from the trail.

Camping, simple lodging: None

Swimming, fishing: None

Winter sports: Cross-country skiing is encouraged. Snowmobiles are prohibited.

Maps, guides, other references

Trail Users' Guide to The Montour Trail. Trail map/brochure available at trailheads and local bike shops.

USGS Topographic Maps: Clinton, Midway, Canonsburg

Montour Trail, South Park Section

Along Piney Fork in South Park Township in Allegheny County

The seed of the South Park section of the Montour Trail has been sown with a mile and a half of trail. It runs beside Piney Fork creek, parallel to Brownsville Rd and Piney Fork Rd. There's currently only one access point, near the Bethel Park and South Park sewer plant on Piney Fork Rd. Access at the endpoints won't be available until bridges are rebuilt.

The west end of this trail segment is on the south side of a bridge over Brownsville Rd near Stewart Rd. This bridge is closed pending reconstruction, and there's no trail access here. The trail is next to a golf driving range here; beware of flying golf balls. Trail fencing has been installed to protect you, so stay on the trail. Aside from the golf area, the trail runs alongside Piney Fork creek for a secluded half-mile to Brownsville Rd Extension, where it crosses at grade.

Another .3 mile brings you to the entrance road for the sewer plant. The 10-car parking lot here is for trail use, and this is currently the only trail access point. After this lot, the road climbs away from the creek and you're left in relative solitude with the woods and the creek. Too soon (in half a mile) the trail ends at a bridge without a deck. Stay off this one until it's re-decked. Triphammer Rd is in sight, crossing the trail alignment on a high embankment. Eventually the trail will cross the bridge and reach Triphammer Rd. Eventually it will be extended at both ends.

Montour Trail, South Park Section	
Location	South Park Township, Allegheny County
Trailheads	Piney Fork Rd
Length, Surface	1.3 miles developed; crushed stone
Character	Little-used, suburban, shady, flat
Usage restrictions	No motorized vehicles; no snowmobiles
Amenities	Food
Driving time from Pittsburgh	45 minutes south

Access points

Vicinity: Directions begin headed south on Clairton Rd (PA51) from its intersection with Library Rd (Blue Belt). To reach this point from Pittsburgh, go south through the Liberty Tubes and turn left on PA51.

Only trailhead (Piney Fork): Follow PA51 to the Yellow Belt and turn right on Curry Hollow Rd (toward South Park). Turn left on Brownsville Rd just after crossing a creek. Follow Brownsville Rd through South Park. Where Brownsville Rd makes a sharp right at Piney Fork Rd (at the CoGo store), turn left on Piney Fork Rd. In 0.5 mile, turn right into trail parking at the entrance to the Bethel Park/South Park waste water treatment plant.

Amenities

Rest rooms, water: None

Bike shop, rentals: West of the trail, on Library Road.

Restaurant, groceries: CoGo at the crossing of Brownsville Rd Extension

Camping, simple lodging: None

Swimming, fishing: None

Winter sports: No snowmobiles.

Maps, guides, other references

Trail Users' Guide to The Montour Trail. Trail map/brochure available at local bike shops.

USGS Topographic Maps: Bridgeville, Glassport

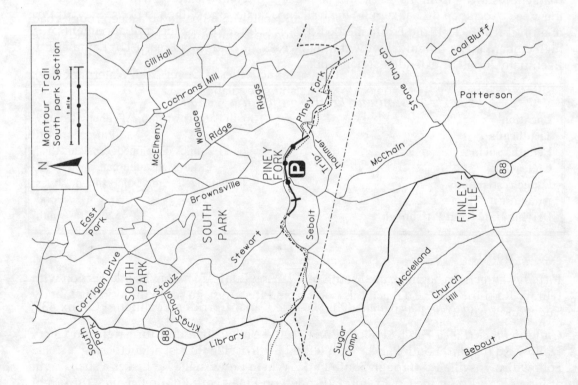

Shorter Trails and Bike Lanes near Pittsburgh

Lawrenceville Trail

From 43rd to 36th Sts in Lawrenceville, City of Pittsburgh

Tucked away behind Lawrenceville industrial plants near the Washington Crossing Bridge, this pleasant trail offers a short walk beside the Allegheny River. Half the trail runs behind the Carnegie Mellon Robotics Consortium; the other half is behind a warehouse. The trail is well above the river, but close to it. Between the trees you'll get a good view of whatever is happening on the river.

Although this trail is currently only 7 blocks long, the Lawrenceville Development Corporation hopes to extend it to 31st St, where it will connect via the 31st St Bridge with the Washington Landing end of the Three Rivers Heritage Trail.

Access point

From downtown Pittsburgh, go east on Penn Ave to 40th St. Turn left on 40th St. Keep right to avoid crossing the Allegheny River on Washington Crossing Bridge. There is parking for a few cars where 40th St ends at the Carnegie Mellon Robotics Consortium.

Downtown to Oakland Riverview Trail

From Downtown Pittsburgh to Greenfield

When completed to Oakland, this off-road commuter trail will connect Allegheny County's two largest employment centers, downtown Pittsburgh and Oakland. It will start from the parking lot near the downtown Grant St Police Station, run behind the jail to another parking lot, then get a clean run of almost two miles between the Parkway and 2nd Av to Hazelwood. Eventually it will turn away from the river and connect to Oakland.

The 2-mile section along the Parkway should be completed late in 1997. The trail will have a 12' paved width, plus additional crushed stone lanes for joggers and walkers. Although it will run between two busy roads, it will have great views. With a cliff on one side, a river on the other, and no cross traffic, we expect this to be a superb trail.

Initially it will end at another parking lot (currently private) on Swinburne St just west of the intersection at the bottom of Greenfield Av, where 2nd Av jogs under the railroad tracks.

Access point

From Grant St in downtown Pittsburgh, enter the public parking lot at the City Court/Police Station. The trail begins under the Port Authority Transit Bridge next to this lot.

Five Star Trail

Parallel to US119 from Greensburg to Youngwood in Westmoreland County

The Five Star Trail is named for the 5 towns that cooperated to develop it: Greensburg, South Greensburg, Southwest Greensburg, Hempfield Township, and Youngwood. When finished, it will parallel US119 from Lynch Field in Greensburg to the Railroad Museum in Youngwood and eventually onward to Westmoreland Community College, running largely through the industrial areas the railroad once served. Because of its urban character and location close to busy US119, this may become foremost a transportation and local recreation trail rather than a major destination.

This trail is unique in western Pennsylvania, in that it shares its corridor with an active rail line. The Southwest Pennsylvania Railroad runs 2-4 coal and freight trains daily. These are mostly short and slow, as trains go, but they still require great caution. Please help make this combination "rail-with-trail" a success by avoiding conflict with the trains. **Stay off the tracks and out of the buffer zone between the trail and the tracks.**

Although only 2.4 miles in two sections is currently finished, the trail is under active development, with another 1.7 miles scheduled for 1997. You may also use unfinished parts of the trail at your own risk. Please be very careful, especially on the unfinished sections and near train tracks.

The trail will eventually begin at Lynch Field in Greensburg. For now, though, the trail begins at the south end of the Pittsburgh St trestle. Here it's finished in crushed limestone for 1.7 miles. It runs for 2 blocks next to Greensburg Shopping Center and residential back yards, then drops onto a bench. Here the hillside rises on the east, punctuated by occasional access stairs and ramps. To the west the ground drops away, providing a great view of central Greensburg. After 0.7 mile, you cross a trestle and enter Southwest Greensburg. Here the trail runs through mixed residential and industrial areas of Southwest Greensburg, then under the Greensburg bypass and into South Greensburg. The finished part of the trail ends at Huff Av (PA819).

Unfortunately, the future trail hasn't been separated from the active rail line for the half-mile from Huff Av to Fairview St. There's not yet a really good way to bypass this half-mile. The best route we've found is to turn west (left) on Huff Av and take the first right on an unnamed alley between the white brick plant building and Cline's auto body shop (this is within sight of the trail). Follow the unnamed alley for 0.5 mile on asphalt, then brick, then gravel. Turn left when the alley ends at Short St, then almost immediately right on Fairview. The trail crosses Fairview in 0.1 mile. This requires less than a quarter-mile on busy streets, but it goes up and down a 40-50' hill.

At Fairview St the wide trailbed resumes. Two trestles over Jack's Run have been rebuilt, and finished surface should be in place by fall 1997. The obligatory waste-water treatment plant (every trail seems to have one!) is just past the second of these trestles. After the water plant, the trail parallels Broadway St, the residential street of Midway. A mile from Fairview St you reach the road crossing at Shady Lane in Midway. It is possible to bypass this section on low-traffic roads to the east (start on Broad St Ext at the Short St-Fairview intersection and follow the pavement to and along Broadway).

After Midway the trail runs through woods beside Jacks Run for 0.7 miles to the entrance to the Buncher Commerce Park. Some safety improvements have been made, and finished surface should be in place by fall 1997. You'll hear both bird song and traffic noise from parallel US119.

The trail emerges at the entry road to the Buncher Commerce Park. The creek has been re-channeled away from the tracks, and the trail route has not yet been established. You can use the low-traffic road that runs between the new creek channel and the warehouses; to do this, turn left where the trail emerges on the road, follow the road along the creek, then turn right a mile later at Mt Pleasant Rd/Depot St.

Where the road leaves the Commerce Park, the creek returns to its original channel and the trail resumes just across the tracks from the Railroad Museum on Depot St. in Youngwood. From here the finished trail continues another half-mile along the track to Hillis Dr/Fairgrounds Rd. Eventually another branch of the trail will lead from this intersection to Westmoreland Community College and beyond.

Five Star Trail	
Location	Greensburg to Youngwood, Hempfield Township
Trailheads	Highland Av near Pittsburgh St, Youngwood
Length, Surface	2.4 miles finished (7.5 miles planned), crushed stone
Character	uncrowded, mixed residential and industrial, shady, flat
Usage restrictions	Stay off RR tracks and out of buffer zone between trail and tracks no motorized vehicles
Amenities	Rest rooms, water, bike rental, food, lodging
Driving time from Pittsburgh	50 minutes southeast

Local history, attractions

Current train traffic along the trail is operated by Southwest Pennsylvania Railroad on the former Conrail Southwest Secondary Branch, which runs from behind Greengate Mall to Connellsville. They operate 2-4 trains a day with 6-10 cars each; these trains shouldn't run faster than 10 mph. Before Conrail took it over, the line was operated by the Pennsylvania RR.

A Railroad Museum at Youngwood is open Tuesday through Saturday from 10:00 AM to 2:00 PM, possibly later on Saturday. This is the north terminus of a scenic passenger railroad.

Access points

Vicinity: Directions begin headed east on the PA Turnpike from Exit 6 (Monroeville). To reach this point from Pittsburgh, take the Parkway East past Monroeville.

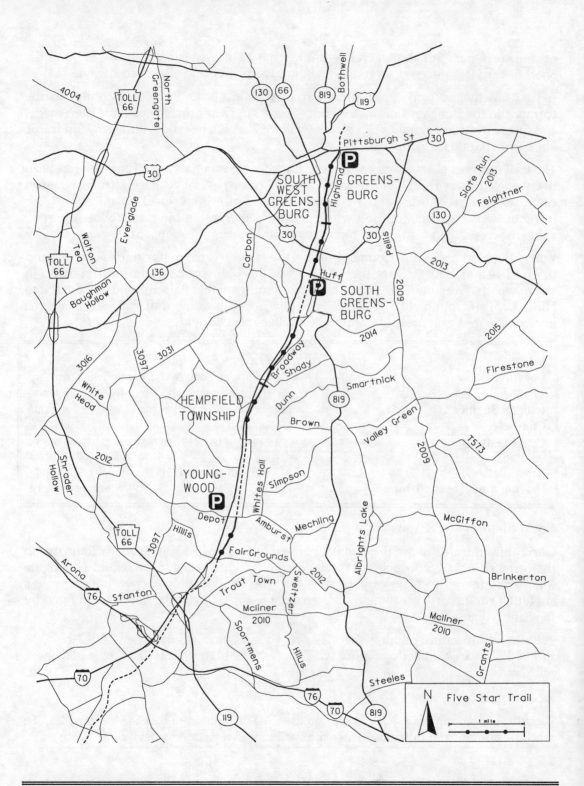

Highland Av near Pittsburgh St trailhead: Get off the Pa Turnpike at Exit 7 (Irwin) headed east on US30 toward Greensburg. Go east 6.4 miles on US30 and take the Pittsburgh St exit. This is the first Greensburg exit, just past Greengate Mall. Go 1.6 miles on Pittsburgh St, passing the county courthouse, an ornate stone building with a gold dome. A third of a mile after the courthouse, you pass under a railroad trestle. Immediately after the trestle and before the Greensburg Shopping Center, turn right on Highland St and look for inoffensive parking. The ramp up to the trail is about a block down Highland St, across from a cleaning shop.

Youngwood (south) trailhead: Get off the Pa Turnpike at Exit 8 (New Stanton) following signs to go north on US119 toward Greensburg. After a mile and a quarter of highway interchanges, you'll be on US119 entering Youngwood. In a few blocks US119 splits, with the northbound lanes a block away from the southbound lanes. Continue for .6 miles after the split to the Depot St traffic light and turn right on Depot St. This is the fourth traffic light in Youngwood; the street sign may be missing, but it's marked as the turn for the community college. Go two blocks on Depot St to the Railroad Museum; the trail and parking are just past the tracks at the museum.

Amenities

Rest rooms, water: In Lynch Field

Bike shop, rental: Bike shops in Greensburg

Restaurant, groceries: Many restaurants along US119. Lots of chain fast food places near Huff Av. Barbecued chicken and ribs on weekend afternoons at the Railroad museum. Convenience stores within a few blocks of Lynch Field and the Railroad Museum.

Camping, simple lodging: Motels in the Greensburgs and Youngwood, including one adjacent to the trail near Huff Av.

Swimming, fishing: Jacks Run is a bilious shade of grayish green, running over orange rocks. We doubt that fish live there, and we certainly aren't about to swim in it. There's a swimming pool at Lynch Field.

Trail organization

Brian Zadorecky
Five Star Trail Council of the Regional Trail Corporation
RD12 Box 203
Greensburg PA 15601
(412) 830-3959
Membership: $15/year individual, $20/year family

Maps, guides, other references

Trail brochure

USGS Topographic Maps: Greensburg, Mount Pleasant

Wheeling Heritage Trails

Along Ohio River from Pike Island Dam to South Wheeling with spur along Wheeling Creek from Wheeling to Elm Grove in Ohio County WV

Located in the northern panhandle of West Virginia, this trail is almost in western Pennsylvania. It's a Y-shaped asphalt-paved trail with a main stem of 8.5 miles along the Ohio River and a partly-finished 4.7-mile spur eastward along Wheeling Ck to Elm Grove. The core of the trail lies in urban Wheeling, and its three legs reach out into the suburbs and beyond. We're used to meeting friendly people along trails, and the folks here were particularly congenial.

The main stem of the trail runs from Pike Island Lock and Dam, 6 miles north of Wheeling, to 48th St in South Wheeling. The setting varies from open countryside to downtown park. All along, you have superb views of the Ohio River. Pike Island Lock and Dam provides an observation deck from which you can watch boat traffic on the Ohio River pass through the locks. The trail starts here in open countryside within sight of WV2. Soon you enter the residential community of Warwood, where many of the yards beside the trail are attractively landscaped. The residential setting gives way to light industry, then the trail returns to parallel WV2. There are a few restaurants here; the one 4.7 miles from Pike Island has tables beside the trail for you to eat pizza and subs. Several side roads cross the trail in this area. In contrast to the practice on many trails, the trail traffic has the right of way; vehicle traffic must stop. There are two 10' hills where the trail jogs from the former railroad grade to highway level to go around obstacles.

You soon enter North Wheeling and cross under I70, 5.7 miles from Pike Island. Immediately afterward, you go under the historic Wheeling Suspension Bridge. This was the longest bridge in the world when it was constructed in 1849. It was also the first bridge across the Ohio River, serving as "gateway to the west"; when it opened, the toll was 10 cents for a man and a horse. It is now a National Civil Engineering Landmark, a National Historic Landmark, and the most significant pre-Civil war engineering structure in the country. The trail here is below street level, with the Ohio River on one side and a stone wall on the other. Frequent stairs and ramps provide access to local businesses. After the suspension bridge, you go through a small park beside the waterfront amphitheater, pass the parking garage at 12th St that serves as the Wheeling trailhead, and enter the park in front of the Civic Center. The downtown section is lighted for night use. Leaving the park, the trail leads between the Civic Center and the Ohio River to the mouth of Wheeling Creek, 6.2 miles from Pike Island. Eventually the spur trail up Wheeling Creek will connect here.

The main trail crosses Wheeling Creek on a wood-decked bridge and continues down the Ohio River through Center Wheeling. At first you're in a former railroad yard with some light industry, then you pass a waste water treatment plant (a standard feature of rail-trails), and then you go under the I470 bridge. South of I470 you're in South

Wheeling. Here the trail is mostly residential -- you even ride through far right field of the local ball field. The trail ends in a small parking lot at 48th St, next to Captain Ed's Floating Lounge.

The spur trail up Wheeling Creek is known as East Wheeling Trail. It will eventually connect with the main trail at the mouth of Wheeling Creek. For now, there's a .65-mile gap on city streets. To connect with the finished parts of the trail, go through the parking lot between the Civic Center and Wheeling Creek, then pick your way through streets and parking lots parallel to Wheeling Creek (directly away from main trail). Try to stay between 16th St (which is pretty busy) and the creek, aiming for the intersection of 17th St and Wood St. The finished trail begins here, running on a bench above limited-access US250. After a block behind residences, the trail crosses a trestle and shares a short gorge with the creek and the highway. Soon the trail swings over the highway and creek and enters a tunnel -- one of the few lighted tunnels in this area. You emerge from the tunnel alongside the creek and I70. After 1.3 miles, the trail ends on Rock Point Rd. To reach the other finished segment, follow Rock Point Rd for .35 miles, turn right at the "T" with Mt De Chantel Rd, and follow Mt De Chantel Rd for .3 miles to its intersection with Washington Av just before it crosses I70. There's not much traffic on this connection except at the last intersection. The finished trail resumes at this intersection (don't cross I70) and continues for 2.1 miles to Elm Grove. The highway crosses to the other side of the creek and exercise stations of a Parcourse appear beside the trail. The highway becomes unobtrusive, though you don't escape its billboards. For now, the trail ends at a dead end street at the edge of Elm Grove.

	Wheeling Heritage Trails
Location	Along Ohio River and Wheeling Creek in Richland, Triadelphia, and Ritchie Townships and cities of Wheeling and Bethlehem, WV
Trailheads	Elm Grove, Wheeling, Pike Island Dam
Length, Surface	8.5 miles along Ohio River, plus segments of 1.3 and 2.1 miles along Wheeling Creek, asphalt
Character	busy, urban, sunny, flat
Usage restrictions	No motorized vehicles, no horses
Amenities	Rest rooms, water, bike rental, food, fishing
Driving time from Pittsburgh	1 hour 20 minutes southwest

Access points

Vicinity: Directions begin headed westbound on I70 at the Pa-WV state line. To reach this point from Pittsburgh, go south on I79 to Washington PA, then west on I70.

East trailhead (Elm Grove): From the Pa-WV state line, continue west on I70 for 9 miles to Exit 5, Elm Grove, and exit southbound on WV 88/91. Go about half a mile on WV88/91 to Junior Av, across from the Elm Terrace shopping center. Turn right on Junior Av. Go 0.2 miles on Junior Av and turn left on Lava Av. This is the third left, just as you reach a school. Continue .4 miles on Lava Av and cross over to the unfinished trail to park.

Downtown Wheeling: From the Pa-WV state line, continue west on I70 for 13.5 miles to Exit 1A, WV2, and exit southbound on WV 2. To make this exit gracefully, be in the right lane as you enter the tunnel and take the exit at the west end of the tunnel. Follow signs to Downtown; you'll be on Main St. Continue to 12th St. Turn right on 12th St. You'll see a parking garage straight ahead. You cross the trail just before entering the parking garage.

North trailhead (Pike Island Lock and Dam): From the Pa-WV state line, continue west on I70 for 13.5 miles to Exit 1A, WV2, and exit northbound on WV 2. To make this exit gracefully, be in the right lane as you enter the tunnel and take the exit at the west end of the tunnel. Follow signs for Pike Island; you'll wind up northbound on WV2. Follow WV2 for 6 miles to Pike Island Lock and Dam; turn left into the parking lot. The dam is easy to spot from a distance because of the overhead structure.

Amenities

Rest rooms, water: Rest rooms and water at the Pike Island Lock and Dam overlook. Portajohns at several ball fields within sight of the trail.

Bike shop, rental: Rentals beside the trail in a shop near 11th St and sometimes in the park near 14th St in downtown Wheeling.

Restaurant, groceries: This is, for the most part, an urban trail. There are many places to get food within a few blocks of the trail. The most convenient is Bartoli's, a pizza/sub shop with tables beside the trail 1.3 miles north of the amphitheater in downtown Wheeling.

Camping, simple lodging: Many motels near Wheeling.

Swimming, fishing: Fishing in Ohio River and Wheeling Creek. We have no information on water quality in Wheeling Creek.

Trail organization

Heritage Trail Partners
Department of Development
1500 Chapline St, Room 305
Wheeling WV 26003
(304) 234-3701

Maps, guides, other references

Trail brochure

Adventure Guide to WV Rail Trails, from the WV Rails-to-Trails Council, PO Box 8889, South Charleston, WV 25303-0889, (304) 722-6558.

USGS Topographic Maps: Tiltonsville OH-WV, Wheeling WV-OH

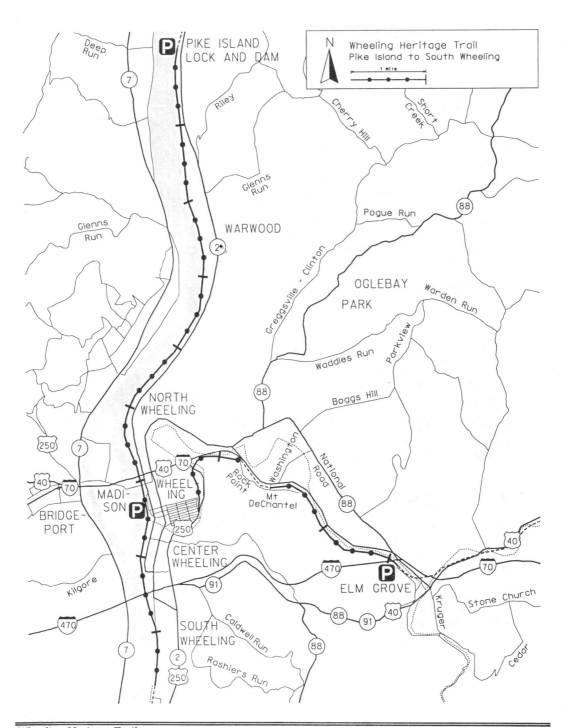

Deep Run

P PIKE ISLAND LOCK AND DAM

Riley

Cherry Hill

Short Creek

N Wheeling Heritage Trail
Pike Island to South Wheeling
1 mile

7

Glenns Run

Pogue Run

88

WARWOOD

2

Glenns Run

Greggsville - Clinton

OGLEBAY PARK

Warden Run

Waddles Run

Parkview

Boggs Hill

88

NORTH WHEELING

Washington

National Road

Rock Point

250 7

40 70

40 70

WHEEL ING

MADI-SON P

40 70

BRIDGE-PORT

250

Mt DeChantel

88

88

40

Kilgore

CENTER WHEELING

470

P ELM GROVE

70

91

Stone Church

Kruger

91

470

SOUTH WHEELING

Caldwell Run

88

91 40

Cedar

7

2

250

Rashiers Run

88

Index to Trails